Sir Walter
The Earl of Chatham

or

Call Your Next Case

❖❖❖❖❖❖❖❖❖❖❖

By H. F. [Chub] Seawell, Jr.

This is a semi-automatic biography with proven
provincialisms, colloquialisms, inter-nationalisms,
some misspellings and bad English, accidentally
and on purpose by the author.

HERITAGE HOUSE

CHARLOTTE

Drawings by W. G. Hargis

Photographs follow page 58

FORE-WORD

(Which is always better than 'hind word)

"Of writin' books there ain't no end, and too much study is a weariness of the flesh."

This book is not written in praise of the flesh. The last report that I had concerning the flesh was that it was mighty weak. Squire Jesse Frye used to say, "How fast the world advances; how little man improves." On the one hand are the marvels of television, jet planes, air conditioning, electronics — on the other are wars without end, murder, cheating, stealing, and other crimes too numerous to mention.

No man ought to think too highly of himself, *but according as God has dealt to him the measure of Faith.*

Some folks don't have any better sense than to write a book, but this book is written to cheer folks up. The Lord himself said one time, "Be of good cheer."

CALL YOUR NEXT CASE.

H. F. "Chub" Seawell, Jr.

Carthage, N. C.
March 10, 1959

There are three things which are real: God, human folly, and laughter. Since the first two pass our comprehension, we must do what we can with the third.

AUBREY MENEN

1

SIR WALTER was born in the great state of Chatham County, North Carolina, which is as good a place as there is in the world to be born, if you've got to be born, not unlessen it is Moore County where I was born. One of the most beautiful things about Chatham County is that it is completely surrounded by North Carolina. On the northeast side flows the Haw River, on the southwest the Deep River. They both come together and form the great Cape Fear River, up the valley of which came such notable, lovable and outrageous characters as John A. Oates and Flora MacDonald, flanked by the McLeods, the McNeills, the McQueens, the McRaes, and other God-blessed Macs too

numerous to mention, to say nothing of Judge Quincy
Nimocks and Oscar Breece. Time would fail me to tell
of the Blues and the Johnsons and the Clarks and the
Shaws and the Roses and the multitudinous other
Scotch folks living in the golden city of Fayetteville.

Sir Walter told me one time that in the olden days
folks used to hitch up their wagons and drive down
from Chatham to trade at Fayetteville. It usually took
several days of camping in the covered wagon. He said
a couple left Chatham one day and went down to trade.
They visited all the stores and then about dark went up
on Hay Mount above town to camp. After they got a
fire going and the horses unhitched the old lady sat
down on a stump to look over her bills, while the pots
in the fire were getting hot. She read a statement about
calico, gingham, and other items and finally she struck
an item marked "ditto."

She jumped up and said, "Old man, them merchants
at Fayetteville are cheating the eyeballs outen us. I
never bought nary bit of ditto—charging me with ditto
when I never bought none! Get on that horse and go
down there and set them merchants straight."

He hopped on his horse and rode off, and she continued to fuss and cuss about being charged with
"ditto" when she never bought nary bit of it. Pretty
soon the old man appeared over the hill, coming back,
and she put her hand to her mouth and hollered: "Old
man, what did you find out?"

He replied in the same tone: "I found out I'm a damn fool and you're a 'ditto'."

As I said before, Sir Walter was born in the great state of Chatham County. After a while I will tell you when, but right now it doesn't make much difference. The thing about it was, he was certainly born, and he was kin to the Joneses who are a multitude of people, including such characters as John Paul Jones (after whom a liquor has been named), and Bobby Jones, the lawyer from Atlanta, who in later days followed President Ike around watching him try to play golf and talk with Dulles at the same time.

It is a pity that Sir Walter and Will Rogers couldn't have lived until these days; their comments would have been a great help to a number of folks who always take themselves so seriously and appear on the scene looking like they were born in crab-apple season and put up in vinegar. It is probably a good thing though that both of them died before we entered these strenuous times. The comments they could have made about foreign policy, farm policy and policy in general, and the magnificent foolishness of politics, could have brought on many a convulsion.

Sir Walter was a past master at satire. He knew history, but he was also up to the minute with current events. He saw what was going on and could collect it and spread it out and then stir it up and mix it with sarcasm and ridicule in a highly satisfactory manner.

Those who know North Carolina know the Dukes, the American Tobacco Co., the Reynoldses, and Prince Albert, and Camels, and how they have done some considerable endowing. One time, Judge Hoyle Sink was holding court over in Randolph County. The courthouse was full of folks, all scared to breathe, mostly. Judge Sink, who has a magnificent sense of humor (when you know him), was sitting on the bench in all his dignity, looking as cold and stiff as a firepoker in August, when all of a sudden Sir Walter appeared at the back door of the courtroom and took a stance in the door looking like a cross between Napoleon and George Washington.

Judge Sink looked up, and seeing him, said, "Here is Judge Walter Siler. I wonder what he wants with the court this morning. Come in Judge Siler."

Sir Walter walked down the aisle with his hat on one arm and his cane on the other. The courtroom full of folks got right still. Sir Walter walked up to the bench, and when he got himself in position in front of the Judge he bowed down real low and said, in his deep bass voice; "GOOD MORNING, MY LORD."

Judge Sink said, "Good morning Judge Siler. Do you have any business with the court?"

"Yes, Your Honor. I desire to make a motion."

"Well, what is your motion, Judge Siler?"

Stepping back a few feet so all could hear, and putting on a very serious and dignified tone of voice, Sir Walter said: "If it pleases Your Honor, I point out to the court that the American Tobacco Company have taken over the er- er, Methodists; the R. J. Reynolds Tobacco Company have taken over the Baptists; this goose-grease Vick's croup and pneumonia crowd up about Greensboro have taken over the Presbyterians. I move the court, Sir, that at least one distillery of Lord Calvert be allotted to the Episcopalians."

Everybody in the courtroom roared, knowing what was going on in North Carolina. But Judge Sink frowned up with one of his de luxe frowns. The courtroom got still as death. Some got to whispering, "He's going to fine him; might even put him in jail."

Finally Judge Sink spoke these beautiful words: "Judge Siler, the court thinks your motion is a timely motion, and your motion is granted."

Whereupon Judge Siler bowed low again and said, "Thank you, My Lord," and departed out the side door.

If I could just have had a talking picture machine hidden in the courthouse where I could have gotten this incident recorded and put on film, I could have made a million dollars with it and wouldn't have had to write this book.

CALL YOUR NEXT CASE.

2

SIR WALTER SILER was born in Siler City, which is the Gotham of Chatham County. He was born on the 25th day of November, 1878. His father was Alson R. Siler and his mother was Nannie Jones Siler. He had three sisters, Mrs. Lula Williams, Miss Helen and Miss Stella Siler, and two brothers, Claude W. and Gordon L. Siler.

His father and mother, in addition to being well educated, had an unusual amount of good old-fashioned sense and there is no doubt but that a great deal of this good sense was handed down to Sir Walter. He told me one time that the word Siler meant rope maker, and with the usual twinkle in his eye he said that it was not the making of rope that hurt folks, it was the giving of enough of it whereby many folks got hung.

This reminded him of the man who five times ran for the Legislature, got beat every time and so decided to end it all. He bought himself a rope, some kerosene

oil, some matches, and some "rough on rats" poison
and went down to Deep River and got a boat and
moved out under the limb of a tree. He tied the rope
around his neck and hung it over the limb. Then he
swallowed the "rough on rats." Then he anointed his
head with kerosene oil, struck a match, and set himself
on fire. He pulled out his pistol to shoot himself in the
head, but his foot slipped and the pistol shot the rope
in two. He fell out of the boat into the water and it
put the fire out. He got strangled when he went under
the water and got rid of the "rough on rats." As he
came to himself while sitting in the shallow water at
the edge of the river, he decided to run for the Legislature again, and this time he was elected.

What some folks won't do to hold public office is a
sight and a caution. Sir Walter told me that was a true
story and maybe it is, mostly.

Sir Walter was married in the year 1921 to Miss Lida
Alston of Chatham County, who died in 1928. The
Alstons were prominent folks in Chatham and Moore
Counties and they wouldn't have anything to do with a
man named David Fanning, although they did have to
surrender to him over on Deep River when he threat-
ened to burn down the house. The Alstons were great
Patriots, and if there ever was anything that Sir Walter
loved, it was a Patriot. He used to go up and down
Deep River with Congressman W. C. Hammer making
patriotic speeches, both of them seeing which one could
cut out David Fanning the best. It was quite a close
contest at times. They both knew how to spread the

language with considerable force and style and when
the Fourth of July crowds would do a little clapping
they would really let go with black powder from both
barrels.

No man ever lived in the great state of North Carolina who could really use satire and humor like Sir
Walter. After cussing out David Fanning or some other
enemy of Revolution days, he would end up with a
great tirade about why he would know that no such
person could be a Rotarian or a Kiwanian or Lion or
belong to the Jaycees.

Sir Walter did not have any children and he told me
that at times this made him feel sort of melancholy and
sad, but then it had its cheerful side, because he knew
he was not adding anything to the sin and confusion
of a coming generation.

Sir Walter was a member of the Hickory Mountain
Methodist Church but he never did let this interfere
with his religion. He often told me that most churches
would be better off if they operated on fines and for-
feitures instead of taking up collections. If all church
members who took a drink of liquor were fined, the
church would not only have enough money to operate
on, they would have to install a committee for investing
surplus funds. He used to say that when misconduct
occurred in the church the parties involved should be
put under bond. Then if the trouble happened again,
the bond could be forfeited and this would add considerable to the church surplus fund.

One of the longest trials ever conducted in Randolph

County was a church dispute in which Sir Walter appeared. The trial lasted two weeks and Sir Walter spoke for about six hours. He enjoyed it more than any case he ever appeared in, even better than the Strickland case in Texas. When you try a church case you have such a wide variety of things to talk about.

No church case has ever been tried where the point involved in the case even got into the issues to be submitted to the jury. Most parties involved, and especially the large and overwhelming majority of the court officials, lawyers, judges, and jurors, *have never been born again, and they are in their natural state and the natural man receiveth not the things of the Spirit of God, for they are foolishness unto him. Neither can he know them because they are spiritually discerned,* therefore in nearly every church case in court it is a matter of the blind leading the blind, and usually both sides fall into the ditch. Scripture admonishes Christians not to go to law before the unjust, but they do it sometimes in spite of all admonishing. When it happens, the devil has a field day, and all born-again, saved Christians suffer in silence while the foolishness rolls on to nowhere.

While speaking to the jury in the Asheboro case, Sir Walter, in referring to one of the witnesses in the case, said: "Gentlemen of the jury, I would not say that this witness would dare put his hand on the Holy Evangel of Almighty God and swear to a lie, and I would not dare to accuse him of this. But I will say that I have made some observations in this case, and I believe that he would walk barefooted seven miles across the hot sands of Mesopotamia just in order to get to shake hands with Judas Iscariot and ask him to give his kindest regards to Ananias and Saphira."

It was little skitches like this that pleased the whole court, whether they paid any attention to them or not, and Sir Walter loved to give them out. No one was more pleased than he. It reminded him of the time, many years back, when all the preachers met and decided that they would vote on who was the best preacher, the one they had rather hear preach. Each one gave out with his version of who was best until they came to an oldtimer with a long beard. After giving his beard a few strokes with his hand he said, "Gentlemen, when I am *right*, I believe I had rather hear myself." This is sad but true of a multitude of folks who do public speaking. When a man gets in love with the sound of his own voice he is hard to stop, especially if he is a judge, a lawyer, or a preacher.

Sir Walter also told me about the old-time preachers over in Chatham County who decided one day that a certain preacher should be unfrocked and stopped from his preaching. Finally one old brother asked to be heard and he said, "I just want to ask one question: Does he take up collection?" They all replied that he certainly did. "Well," he said, "let the brother preach on."

Which reminds me of the one Sir Walter told about the church back in the depression days that got considerable behind with the preacher's salary, and he was beginning to complain to the folks for not keeping his salary paid. So a kindly old lady went to him and said that she did not have any money but could furnish him with all the buttermilk he could use. But he more or less brushed her off by saying in stern tones, "Madam, I cannot pay my bills with buttermilk."

"Well," she said, "that is all I have. I don't have any money."

After a few weeks had gone past the men of the church got together and paid off the preacher in full, and he was feeling very happy about the whole matter. He was strolling down the street in a jovial mood when he saw the kindly old lady approaching, and when she got close enough to speak he lifted his hat and bowed real low and in a most gracious manner said, "Madam, you can let the buttermilk come."

Human nature is interesting to watch. In fact, of all the human beings I ever met, folks are the most interesting people.

CALL YOUR NEXT CASE.

3

SIR WALTER SILER became mayor of Siler City at the ripe age of twenty-one. He began to practice law about 1900, and in 1903 was elected to the House of Representatives, from Chatham County. Some time along about 1910 he was elected solicitor of what used to be the old Fourth Judicial District of North Carolina, and he held this position for some ten years. Then he served as, what he called, a "Bevo" Superior Court judge. A Bevo judge, like Bevo Beer, had considerably limited powers. Later he served as assistant attorney general of North Carolina and as recorder county judge of Chatham.

It was while serving in these capacities that Sir Walter was able to give full play to his love of satire and humor. He would attend all political meetings in the state and especially meetings of the bar, or any meeting about anything concerning public opinion or interest. By attending these meetings he became an expert at pointing out with absolute clarity the total un-importance of almost everything. He told me one day that he was worried sick, what with Mr. Josephus Daniels always attending the State Democratic Convention with his pockets loaded down with resolutions. "There is not but one thing worse than a resolution," he said, "and that is a motion to pass one."

Sir Walter said to me one day, "Seawell, did you ever attend one of those meetings up about Asheville and White Sulphur Springs, that they call the Judicial Conference of the Fourth Federal Circuit?"

I allowed to him that I had, a time or two. "Well," he said, "it is certainly one of the most magnificent pieces of carryin's on that the bar and judges have put on in a long time. Judge John J. Parker very graciously calls the meeting to order, and then he tells what a great and magnificent lawyer, jurist and justice, Chief Justice Vinson is. And then Chief Justice Vinson gets up, but he doesn't get up fast, he gets up kind of slow and in sections like a chain, and he is the wisest looking man you ever saw—he just seems to ooze jurisdiction—and the legal circles under his eyes are so big his nose looks like it's riding a bicycle, and he tells what a great judge Judge Parker is. And then Judge Parker gets that international gleam in his eye, and both of them get up and shake hands and tell what a great lawyer Kenneth Royall is, and then Kenneth gets up and admits it. Of course Kenneth doesn't mean to admit it, but it sort of comes natural with him."

This little story has been told many times in the presence of Judge Parker and Kenneth Royall, and nobody ever enjoyed it any more than they did. No judge ever lived in North Carolina who was more honored, loved and respected than Judge John J. Parker, and the lawyers of North Carolina have given to Kenneth Royall the highest honor they can bestow. I wish Sir Walter was still living, he could most likely get up something new on them by this time.

The New Deal didn't set so well with Sir Walter, and although a staunch Democrat, he often stated that some of the things that Mr. Roosevelt did were as improper as taking carbolic acid to cure the indigestion—one dose was truly sufficient. One of Sir Walter's chief complaints was the failure of Mr. Roosevelt to appoint a Gourd Board. This would have been a great and wonderful field of endeavor because there could have been appointed two special Gourd Commissions, one on long-handled gourds and one on short-handled gourds, and then of course attorneys could have been appointed to both groups and they could have broken up into other groups and then the lawyers, through the attorney general, could have developed some expert attorneys in the field of long-handled and short-handled gourds.

A Gourd Board operating in the proper manner of cooperation with the Department of Agriculture could have paid farmers not to raise long-or-short-handled gourds and the depression might have been overcome and it would not have been necessary to go through World War II in order to bring on our false prosperity. And most likely the United Nations would not have been necessary.

At the time when the Supreme Court of the United States was being overwhelmingly packed with men yet unheard of in the realms of jurisprudence, Sir Walter said to me, "Seawell, the next time there is a vacancy on the Supreme Court, I have in mind a special man I desire to receive the appointment. It's Squire Dade over in Raleigh."

"I have never heard tell of him," I remarked.

"Well," he says, "that is one of the first qualifications. But that ain't all. He is not just an ordinary justice of the peace, he is a sort of cosmopolitan justice of the peace. He not only tries cases around Raleigh, he goes down around Goldsboro and Wilmington and tries cases clean out of his jurisdiction. But the most important thing about him is that just a few days ago he was apprehended—I don't like that word caught—over in the Sir Walter Hotel in a room with a woman of considerable pre-possessing characteristics, and rather than have any *News and Observer* reports of the usual nature, he just called in another justice of the peace and married the woman.

"Well," I asked, "what in the world has that got to do with a man being appointed to the Supreme Court of the United States?"

"Now THAT," replied Sir Walter, "is the most important part of the qualification. It proves conclusively that he is a LIBERAL."

One day as Sir Walter and I rode down Constitution Avenue in Washington, D.C., he said, "Seawell, stop the car. Do you hear that rattling noise?"

"Yes Judge, what is it?" I asked.

"Little men up here trying to sit in big seats," replied Sir Walter.

CALL YOUR NEXT CASE.

4

SIR WALTER would enjoy reading this book because he would know that what I am saying is the truth, mostly. One of the most enjoyable things about being honest is that you don't have to bother about telling lies. Dr. William L. Pettingill used to say that people ought to quit giving excuses about things, because usually an excuse was just a reason stuffed into the skin of a lie.

One of the biggest lies ever put in circulation is often referred to as "World Federation and Everlasting Peace." About the time that this subject was much in vogue, Sir Walter was asked to make an address at Pine-hurst to a cosmopolitan group gathered at the Carolina Hotel. Many expected him to follow the usual pattern and make some kind of magnificent address that would most likely change the whole course of civilization. There was consternation and utter disillusionment when he announced that his subject would be "The Groundhog."

Sir Walter told me one time that a certain highly educated gentleman had retired and was being asked about over the country to make speeches. He knew what the man's subject would be, and sure enough, in a few days the papers announced that he was to make an address to a distinguished and learned group on the subject "World Federation and Everlasting Peace." "So I decided I would like to see just how the gentleman would handle his subject," Sir Walter told me. "And this was what he said: 'If everybody would be a Christian and live up to it, and everybody agree not to go to war and abide by it, we would have everlasting peace.' When I read that, I went right home and got out my big record book and put it down under the heading 'Great Minds at Work'."

Those who know anything at all about the truth know that there can be no lasting peace until the Lord comes back and the Government shall be upon His shoulder. Yet and still, we see multitudes listening to highly educated leaders trying to bring world federation and everlasting peace, but who won't mention the name of Jesus.

Sir Walter never did let religion discourage him any, because he never took much stock in forms and ceremonies. He said one time that an old Negro named Uncle Eben died up in Chatham. Uncle Eben was a highly respected old man and widely known, and when it was learned he was dead, it was decided that there should be a great funeralization over him. So folks gathered in great multitudes in the little church down in the lane. Uncle Eben had had the "authoritus" and was kind of bent and when they put him in the coffin and got his head down his feet would fly up. And when they got his feet down his head would fly up. So they got some old cotton strings and tied Uncle Eben down.

Next day the preacher began to funeralize over Uncle Eben, and after about two hours, it was decided to open up the coffin and let folks pass by and get one last look at Uncle Eben. When about one-fourth of the congregation had passed by, the old strings broke and Uncle Eben popped right up in the coffin. Brethren went out the windows and doors and some through the side of the church, and the preacher got around in front of the crowd and was leading the flock up the old lane at a high rate of speed when someone hollered, "Preacher, wha're ya goin'?" Looking back over his shoulder he called, "I ain't a-goin' nowhar, I'm *comin' from* a place."

Sir Walter didn't catch pneumonia sitting around in damp churches listening to preachers "bringing in the Kingdom," because he knew that the Kingdom would not be brought in but would be set up by the Lord

Himself, and he also knew that when he saw a new heaven and a new earth it would be made by the Lord and not by man.

Sir Walter and my uncle, George W. McNeill, were about the same age. Both began law practice about 1900, the same year Judge L. R. Varser began to practice law and the same year Dr. J. Clyde Turner began to preach. My uncle descended from a long line of blue stocking, dyed-in-the-wool Presbyterians, but he was known as my drinking uncle. Sir Walter told me about being in his office one day when he had had a drink or two, and as they descended the stairs of the building out into the street it was apparent that he was about three sheets to the leeward. As my uncle stepped out into the street, he came face to face with Dr. Golden, pastor of the Presbyterian church. Sir Walter said it was too late to back up, and it would have been very bad manners to try to dodge around, so he said Uncle George just stuck out his hand and shook hands with the preacher and said, "Dr. Golden, I'm mighty glad to see you (which wasn't so, but sounded good). You know, I'm a mighty poor Christian, but I'm a powerful Presbyterian."

I asked Sir Walter what happened after that, and he said it looked to him "like they had a fellowship meeting right there on the street."

After I had been making a few talks in different churches over the country, an old friend of mine at Carthage who was also a Presbyterian, used to chide me about it. One day, out on the street in the midst of a group of folks, he said if I didn't quit it he was going to give me a nickname, and everybody would begin to call me "Herbert, The Holy Roller."

"Well," I said, "everybody that's any account usually gets a nickname. There was old William the Conqueror, Richard the Lion Hearted, John the Baptist, and Pilate the Presbyterian."

"Pilate won't no Presbyterian," my friend objected.

"I'm not so sure about that," I replied. "Didn't he hold public office, and wasn't he a politician, and didn't he take a little bowl of water and try to sprinkle around with it?"

Turning his head to one side and looking up at me out of the corner of his eye, he remarked in all seriousness, "I bedogged if you ain't got a point."

Which reminds me of what Sir Walter told about the two Presbyterian elders who attended a great fellowship meeting at old Bethesda Church. All the different denominations showed up and each man was asked to sign a card and give the name of his denomination. One of the old elders signed his card but didn't put down his denomination, and the other one asked him why he didn't give his denomination. "I didn't know how to spell Presbyterian," he answered.

"You could have put down a P."

"Oh, no!" he said. "I was afraid to risk that. Somebody might think I was a 'Piscopalian."

Two colored brethren, according to Dr. Forrest of Toccoa, Ga., were standing on the street talking, and one used the word "procrastination," and the other one said, "Man, what you usin' big words like that for, you don't even know what that word procrasteratin means."

"Why *sho'* I does know what it means. It's one of the main doctrines of the Presbyterian church."

An old Presbyterian of considerable distinction delivered a note to my uncle for collection. After looking at the note, my uncle informed him that it was barred by the statute of limitations and could not be collected. "Well," he said, "I don't care about no statute of limination. All I know is he ain't paid narry cent on this note and I want to judgment him."

After it was explained to him that the note could not be sued on because of the statute, the old gentleman became reconciled. "Ignorance is a simple thing, but damn dangerous," he sighed.

Sir Walter and I often agreed that ignorance is more refreshing and more enjoyable and more entertaining than intelligence, if you have intelligence enough to understand ignorance.

CALL YOUR NEXT CASE.

5

SIR WALTER knew North Carolina and his native Chatham as well as any man that ever lived. He not only knew the past history and the current events, but he knew the personal history of almost every well-known North Carolinian, regardless of race, color, creed or former condition of servitude. With regard to servitude he often said that every judge in North Carolina should serve about six months on the roads so that when he went upon the bench and began to sentence first one and then another he would know more about what he was doing.

North Carolina has been blessed with a great bench

and bar. I have never met a man on the Superior Court bench or the Supreme Court bench that I didn't like. Not only are they all good lawyers, but what I would call cultured and classical gentlemen. It is even doubtful if working on the county roads or serving a jail sentence would do them much good.

Sir Walter loved Chief Justice Walter P. Stacy. Some of the happiest moments of my life were spent in the presence of these two old warriors, listening to their uninhibited "carryin's on." One time down in Monroe a Superior Court decided a matter against Sir Walter and me, and I said, "Judge, what are we goin' to do down here now?"

"Why," he said, "we are right now on our way to see the Chief Justice of North Carolina to get what is known in law as a *supersedeas*. Fill up the car with gas and get me a couple of cigars; times a-wastin'."

So we lit out for Raleigh, some 160 miles distance. We stopped by the office of Judge Varser and prepared our papers, and next day we rolled in to the office of the Chief Justice. When we went into the office, the Chief Justice said, "Gentlemen you look highly disturbed. Walter, what's wrong?"

Whereupon Sir Walter replied, "Mr. Chief Justice, in the words of my old horse-tradin' friend from Chatham County, 'we done and been drove hard and putt up muddy and we don't like it nary bit.'"

The Chief Justice, with the twinkle in his eye for which he was famous, looked over toward me and said, "I know exactly what you 'air a-talkin' about." He signed our *supersedeas*.

Chief Justice Stacy had a brother named Horace Stacy, who was a great and magnificent lawyer. He was also over-endowed with a super-saturated solution of common sense. I introduced him one time to an old Scot from up in Moore County, and after Mr. Stacy had walked off, he turned to me and said, "He's a sleepy-eyed lookin' sort of a fellow, but I bet he can evermore pull wire."

Sir Walter said to me one day, "Seawell, do you know what makes Chief Justice Barnhill such a mean Democrat?"

"Well," I said, "I didn't know he was such a mean Democrat. He has always been mighty nice to me."

"The thing that makes Justice Barnhill such a mean Democrat," replied Sir Walter, "is that his grandfather was a Republican."

"Well," I said, "my grandfather was a Democrat and held office in the Democratic party for forty years."

"In many respects, Seawell, you're one of the meanest Republicans I ever met," he rejoined. It was our happy privilege to compliment each other sometimes beyond any hope of recovery.

Sir Walter and I had a little matter in Charlotte one time, and he always liked to leave early, so we grabbed ten gallons of gas and a couple of cigars for him, and we hit the road about daylight. When we arrived at the courthouse in Charlotte, the janitor was putting some ice water on the desk of the judge in one of the court rooms. I asked him who was holding court and he told me it was Judge Don Phillips. Then I asked him who was holding court over in the other court room. "I don't know, I ain't learnt that judge's name yet. He ain't rowdy like Judge Phillips," he told me.

Sir Walter looked over at me with that little twinkle in his eye and said: "He knows exactly what he is talking about."

"Judge, that is a sort of *rough* appraisal of Judge Phillips, but how would you appraise him?"

"Well," he said, "he is one of the nicest and most likeable and affable of all our Superior Court judges. But he *does* have considerable flavor when he sits down on leather."

One of the nicest things about Judge Phillips is the fact that he loves all these stories they tell on him, and he often repeats them himself. He took me into the office of the clerk of court of Richmond County one day and showed me his picture, which was taken in Germany where he was one of the judges in the trial of the war criminals. He was sitting up on a high bench with black robe on, looking down over the crowded room. He asked me what I thought of it. "I know you want me to be honest Judge, so I'll say this: Goering in his palmiest days never looked any rougher than that."

Sir Walter and I were on the way to court in Asheboro. He would smoke his cigar and read his newspaper while I was doing the driving. Then he would wad up the newspaper and throw it on the floor of the car and look out the window and puff on his cigar. Then he would reach down and unfold the newspaper and read a little more. Then he would wad it up again and cast it to the floor of the car, and puff on his cigar and look out the window. After doing this several times, he said to me: "Seawell, you know we live in a magnificent country, but it seems we've got one of the damn sorriest crowds trying to run it I ever read after."

"Well," I answered, "it does look like we showed partiality about dropping the atomic bomb. We dropped it on the Japanese when it was really the Germans who started this war, and it looks like we were partial about it. We should have dropped at least one bomb over in Germany where this war got started."

"No," he said, "We weren't partial, we evened it all up, because after the war was over we sent Judge Don Phillips over to Germany to try the damn scoundrels and that's worse than the atomic bomb."

Sir Walter said to me one day, "Seawell, I am getting up a list of all the bloody judges of history, and I am in a sort of state of confusion."

"Judge, give me your list and maybe I can help you some," I said.

"Well," he said, "my list goes like this: Pontius Pilate, Herod Antipas, Bloody Jeffers of old England, Clawson L. Williams, and Don Phillips."

"That is a right formidable list, Judge, and it might be hard to improve on," I agreed.

"Yes," he said, "I consider it pretty good, but I have just returned from a session of court down in Richmond County before Judge Don Phillips, and I very much greatly fear I have done Pontius Pilate an injustice."

CALL YOUR NEXT CASE.

6

SIR WALTER loved everybody in Chatham County, but like many folks in public life he also had some enemies. He told me that his enemies tickled him considerable and he enjoyed them very much. This is one of the best ways to treat enemies, but sometimes it makes them madder. Then, if they get mad enough, it brings on a heart attack and they usually get sick and die out and you don't have to bother with them any more.

Sir Walter usually had a good word for everybody, but he did hate self-righteous folks and reformers and what he called innovators. Speaking to the Fourth District Bar Association one time, he said: "There are some things that should be forever safe from the hands of profane cranks and quacks; some institutions that should be beyond the reach of reckless intermeddling and unthinking innovation. If wild-eyed theorists and self-appointed public guardians, and the vast horde that know full well how to manage everybody's business except their own, blind to the lessons of history, are permitted to set at nought these great institutions that have given us national life, let us at least stand fast for the preservation of the multiplication table, the solar system, the law of gravity, Santa Claus, Thanksgiving, Groundhog Day, and the anniversary of the canonization of Elder Frank R. McNinch.

"Old Deal, New Deal, or Misdeal; sitdown strikes, standup strikes, or walkout strikes; third term, fourth term, or put the President under Civil Service, are questions now agitating the public mind. But each in due season will pass as a tale that is told and as a ship in the night.

"However these problems may be solved, the sun will continue to rise and shine and the moon to wax and wane. Men will continue to fall out and fight over politics and religion. Spellbinders will continue to view with alarm and point with pride; wine bibbers will continue to bib, and ardent drys point to bleeding Kansas as the *ne plus ultra* of all the Utopias. But come what may, as far as I am concerned, Appomattox and Reconstruction notwithstanding, I adhere to the theory of

States Rights, and I shall observe Thanksgiving on the day announced by Governor Clyde Hoey."

Governor Hoey was one of North Carolina's most delightful personalities. Having been mixed in with the Republicans all my life, I naturally have heard Lincoln's Gettysburg address at least four million times. Along about February 12th of every year the Republicans learn it all over again and get so they can say it both "back'ards and fo'ards."

Sir Walter asked me one day if I had ever heard Governor Hoey's Salemburg address, *verbatim, et literatim, et punctuatum.*

He said Governor Hoey appeared on the stage at Salemburg with his hair laid back like that of Beethoven, with his longtail coat on and his beautiful carnation in the lapel, and with his hands folded, one resting on the top of the other like an undertaker as they are letting the coffin down. He opened up as follows:

"My fellow North Carolinians, it has been my happy privilege to represent you in the great Congress Halls of the United States for lo these many years. I have recently made a great survey of the great state of North Carolina. I have been down in that great eastern section of North Carolina—that great farming section of North Carolina—and down in eastern North Carolina I see the people of eastern North Carolina going about their daily tasks. And I believe that *the people of eastern North Carolina are a happy people.*

"From there I go to the great Piedmont section of North Carolina. I hear the hum of machinery; I see the great manufacturing plants turning out great quantities of goods to be shipped to all portions of the world and I see the people of Piedmont North Carolina going about their daily tasks and I believe that *the people of Piedmont North Carolina are a happy people.*

"From there I go into the great mountainous sections of North Carolina—that great western section of North Carolina—I see the advancements and improvements being made there in the dairying industry and I see the advancements and improvements being made there in the other industries and I see the people of western North Carolina going about their daily tasks and I believe that *the people of western North Carolina are a happy people.*

"As the poet has so ably sung, 'My country 'tis of thee, sweet land of liberty, of thee I sing. Long may our land be bright with freedom's holy light. *Protect us by thy might, Great God our King.*' "

Then he bows real low and all the people stand up and clap and whisper to each other and say, "Ain't it just beautiful?" and "I never heard anything like that before." And then the women will all smile at each other and gather in little groups and say, "Isn't he magnificent?"

Of course Governor Hoey made this same speech everywhere he went and many people heard it many times, but that didn't make any difference. The way he said it made it seem absolutely fresh and just as if he had never said it before.

It is a pity that a man like Senator Hoey couldn't live to be about two or three hundred years old. The first time I ever saw Senator Hoey was at the funeral of Chief Justice Hoke. I was just a small lad, but I remember that Mr. Hoey was present and he had long hair (it was golden then), and he had on his longtail coat. When I ran for Governor in 1952, Senator Hoey and I bumped into each other at a hot dog stand. We sat on stools up at the counter and had a hot dog and Coca Cola, and he told me some scandalous good stories.

He told one concerning Judge Hoke, who, when he was on the Superior Court bench, was a very impressive man. He had a bass voice that would jar the window panes in the courthouse. When he finished a term, a certain Sheriff came up to him and said, "Judge, you are the best Judge who has ever held court here. You hold court more like a Sheriff than any one I ever saw."

Senator Hoey told me one time that Judge Long was holding court in Shelby one hot spell in June. Where he had to sit in the old courthouse was in a sort of little bay window just back of the bench. There was no way to get any air where he was sitting, so he called for the Sheriff and said, "Sheriff, come, and come quick, and get a saw and a hammer and tear out this window so I can get some air." He stared hard, and asked, "Sheriff, do you want the court to suffocate?"

After the Sheriff got the window out and the Judge started up the proceedings, a little cloud about as big as your hand, or seemed to be, passed over the courthouse square and the lightning flew out of it and knocked a big limb off an elm tree on the courthouse square and the thunder sounded like a cannon fired in the courthouse. The Judge jumped up. "Where in the world is the Sheriff? Sheriff, oh Sheriff," he called, "come, and come quick, and bring your hammer and nails. Close up this window! Do you want the court to be struck by lightning?"

Senator Hoey one time said that when he was a boy he made a speech at a certain gathering, and while standing around after the speaking was over he heard two men talking about his speech in good old southern style, and one man said to the other, "How did you like the speech?"

"The speech won't worth a damn, but his gesticulations was the best I ever saw," replied the other.

CALL YOUR NEXT CASE.

7

SIR WALTER told me about the time he was invited to speak at the State Penitentiary. On the way down he began to think about what he should talk on, and then he got to worrying about how he would start his speech. He was not only at a loss to know what to talk on, he didn't even know how to start. He could not say, "Fellow Citizens," since the prisoners had all had their citizenship taken away from them; he could not say, "Gentlemen," as that would be just a little presumptuous; and he couldn't say, "Friends," because he had helped put most of them in there. So he said, "Boys, what will you have me talk on?" One beetle-browed brother rose up from over on the back side of the crowd and said, "Jedge, we don't care what you talk on just so long as you don't talk on that Prodigal Son, we done heerd to much about him already."

So, sitting at the spring one day up in Chatham County, Sir Walter and I agreed that when you are asked out to talk about something, or address some organization, be they Lions, Tigers, Bears, Elks, Kiwanians, Rotarians, Civitans, Jaycees, or Jay Birds, it is always best to tell what you are *not* going to talk on rather than try to tell what you *will* talk on. Most folks like to be cheered up and when you are invited out to speak, it makes folks feel good to know what you will *not* speak on.

Most speakers when they are asked out to speak always decide within themselves that this would be a good time to demonstrate to their audience their magnificent intelligence. As Andrew H. Brown would say, they try to make an *imprint* on everybody. This is a form of assault. It is not quite an assault and battery but borders on it. Usually you have good food at these meetings, and charming ladies sitting on all sides, and beautiful flowers and decorations. And then up gets some speaker who tries to change the whole course of civilization at one sitting, or tries to impress folks with what he has learned out of some book.

Sir Walter said there is only one other fellow who is more boring than these experts, and that is the fellow who has decided in his own mind that he is a great joke teller, and having never learned the difference between "smutness" and "smartness" he lapses into vulgarity "unbeknownst" to himself. Most folks after hearing of these "smutters" want to put the table cloth over their heads and sneak out the side door. But we praise the Lord that not all speakers are so ignorant of the difference between smutness and smartness. Sir Walter and I agreed that one of the best storytellers this country ever produced was Cyclone Mack, known in and around Chatham and Moore as "Old Cyc," pronounced "Sike."

Cyclone was speaking one time at a revival meeting in Carthage and he said he was going to talk on the "Prodigal Son," and he said he was going to bring the story right down to earth and make it so plain that everybody would understand just what he was talking about. He said he was going to put the Prodigal in modern times and show in plain English just what happened to him so people would understand.

The Prodigal Son, according to Old Cyc, was born in Richmond County, N. C. His father was a rich farmer down in Wolfpit Township. When the Prodigal Son got about grown, he became a Liberal. He wanted to "Go Forward," so he began to beg the old man for his part of the estate before the old man died. He just worried the soul out of the old man, begging for his part. Finally, the old man went up to Rockingham and saw Mr. Leake Conington, the banker, and borrowed $25,000. He gave it to the Prodigal Son, who immediately left Richmond County and went straight in to Chicago.

He landed right at the Palmer House, according to Old Cyc, and he began to have a lot of friends and they put on one cocktail party right after another and all the women sort of took up with him. But after a while the depression hit up there in Chicago, and the Prodigal Son lost all his money, and then he lost all his friends and he got hungry and in awful condition. So he finally got a job out in the stock yards feeding the hogs; and when the man would bring the bran to feed the hogs, the Prodigal Son would reach down in the bag and get a handful of hog feed and eat along with the hogs.

Along in September it began to be pretty cool at night, so when no one was watching, the Prodigal Son would get down in the pen and sleep between two big hogs trying to keep warm. And one night while he was in there between two big hogs, lying on his back looking up at the stars, he got to thinking about his home down in Richmond County. Then Old Cyc would pause dramatically in his story and say: "You know sometimes God puts us on our back so we will look up at Him and quit looking at all these things around us in a sin-cursed world. So the Prodigal said to himself, 'My father has plenty to spare and a good place to live and I am just going back and make myself as a hired man and confess all my sins and just be a servant to the old man.' So, when the L. & N. ran out of Chicago next morning, the Prodigal Son was riding the rods, bumming back to good old Richmond County. He landed home one Sunday morning during a kind of dry hot spell, and he started walking home. The old man was sitting on the front porch reading the *News and Observer* when he looked up the road and saw a speck of dust, and he called to his wife and said, 'Mirandy come here. Ain't that our son a-coming yonder?' "

Old Cyc then told how the old lady reached over and borrowed the old man's glasses and putting them up to her eyes said, "Silas, shore as gun's iron, that's him a-coming."

So the old man said, "Get something to eat around here," and he ran out and met the boy and kissed him and brought him to the house and cleaned him up and put some new clothes on him and then took him into the old dining room and sat him down at the head of the table. And right in front of him they had ham, and sausage, and backbone and spareribs, and bacon, and souse meat and cracklin' bread. And the Prodigal Son looked down at it and taking one hand and brushing it aside said, "I don't want no *hog* meat at all."

A very well known gentleman of Moore County said one time that when he got to heaven he was going to take a stick and break it over the head of the Prodigal Son, not that he had anything against the Prodigal Son but that he had spent about half of his life sitting on hard uncomfortable church benches listening to preachers preach fool sermons about the Prodigal Son. *The love of God has always been beyond the imagination of man. Truly the preaching of the cross is but foolishness to them that perish, but to them that believe, it is the power of God.*

CALL YOUR NEXT CASE.

8

SIR WALTER and I sat down on the banks of the Eno River in the great State of Orange County, North Carolina, and talked history and current events and the general situation as it appeared to us. We finally came to the unanimous conclusion that Prohibition would have been a great success if the liquor hadn't given out. Prohibition was made for the other fellow. Some folks thought that poor folks didn't have any business drinking liquor anyhow. So a lot of cultured drinkers stocked up on liquor and thought it would last a life time, but it soon ran out and cellars went dry. It was discovered that most folks in this country didn't have character enough to obey the law or to enforce it, so a great crusade in the name of Moderation got started and got into politics and caught fire. Then the Devil discovered that he needed to get up a name for taking a drink of liquor, so he got up "cocktail."

A lot of folks get insulted if you offer them a drink of liquor, but everybody will take a cocktail. So when the cocktail got in circulation, we decided that the thing to do would be to clean up the bootleggers and sell liquor ourselves, so we could get money to pay teachers to teach folks not to drink liquor. Which is a reasonable hysteria and seems to state the case.

Both Sir Walter and I having appeared at various times for Will Sanders, we began to review some of Will's mental meanderings. Will was a very highly educated man in an illiterate sort of way. He said to me one day, "Mr. Seawell, I have made more liquor than any other man in North Carolina, 'specially countin' what I made in South Carolina."

"Well," I said, "Will, you must come in contact with Judge Johnson J. Hayes at some time or other."

"Oh, I knows him well. He sent me to Atlanta one time, but he done it in such a genteel way, and so kind, and he explained everything to me so full, I have sort of felt under obligations to him ever since. Of course he grieves me some too, because he takes the liquor business so hard, and just worries over it scandalous. He ought to know that they'll be makin' liquor when he's dead and gone to the glory land."

Will shook his head sadly and continued, "Folks don't seem to have much sense these days, and it's got so now when you go to town, in order to stay there you've got to put a nickel in a stob. Towns have got stobs stuck up all around, and if you don't put in a nickel it costs you a dollar. People ain't got much sense anymore. They're puttin' money in stobs, goin' to ball games and movin' pitcher shows and wastin' their money on all kinds of foolishness when they could be buyin' liquor with it."

Sir Walter said that one time Will told him that he didn't reckon he would ever be a judge, "specially one like Judge Don Phillips. But I'm tellin' you this, if I was a Judge and a man come up before me and was proved that he was a-drivin' his automobile machine 'toxicated, I would consider that a dangerous artillery, and I would provoke his license at once and extend him from driving."

Sir Walter asked Will one day what he thought of Judge Johnson J. Hayes, the first time he saw him holding court. "I knowed when I looked at him," said Will, "that he was a new broom and that he was goin' to try to sweep clean and I had my doubts about him. However, he done better than I thought. First time I seed him he done awful quare. He didn't come into the courthouse and say, 'Sheriff open court,' like a regular judge, but he went way back in a little room and put on a long black-lookin' thing that looked like a nightgown, and he took a little fellow back there with him, and pretty soon both of 'em come walkin' out, and that black thing didn't half fit him and he had to hold it up to keep from steppin' on it, and he come bouncin' along lookin' like Pope Pius the eleventh or the twelfth and that little man was goin' along in front of him, sayin' 'Oh Yes. Oh Yes.' just as if to say, 'I told you so. I told you so.' And then the judge he gets up on that high wide bench-lookin' place, and throws that robe back and looks down over the crowd, just as if to say, *'less than the dust beneath my chariot wheel.'* And then that little man he say, 'Draw Nigh. Draw Nigh.' Draw Nigh hell, what everybody wants to do is run."

Sir Walter said Will told him one time that some of the boys decided to make a little liquor over in the foothills of Chatham. They put themselves up a little ten-gallon still and the first day they operated, a man by the name of Gun Davis caught them making a little run. But he said that he wouldn't report it if they would give him about a pint a day for personal use. So they agreed. But then the old man got to increasing his demands until he wanted about a gallon a day, and they couldn't stand such a drain, as the little still wan't turning out much over a gallon. So they picked up the still and moved over into another little valley to hide from the old man. Next day he came down looking for his payoff and found the still was gone. He went up on the hill and began to call to the boys, shouting, "Boys, where are you? Don't try to fool me. I know you're in here somewheres. Boys, you better answer me!" Finally in desperation the old man said, "Boys, you better answer me. I may not be able to find you, but Johnson J. Hayes can find you!"

Will said they heard the name Johnson J. Hayes, and told the old man to come and get his liquor. But they finally gave up the operation in that territory. And, Will added, that was one liquor operation Judge Hayes broke up without "issuin' nary paper."

Sir Walter and I agreed as we sat by the banks of the old Eno River, that Judge Johnson J. Hayes was one of the finest judges North Carolina will ever produce. He was not only a great lawyer but a gentleman of the old school. Judge Hayes was not only a good judge and lawyer but he was a great speaker. According to Sir Walter, "he could take any kind of subject and play hell with it, and he always combed his subjects with a fine tooth comb."

One of Judge Hayes' best speeches was made at the dedication of the Wake Forest Law School building in the spring of 1957, and with permission, same is made a part of this chapter:

"Law is a living stream whose waters make glad a people who love liberty. It is the task of those who are primarily concerned in the law—teachers, lawyers, law-makers and judges—to keep this stream pure and capable of meeting the demands of an expanding society of enterprising, liberty-loving people.

"Our system of government is founded upon the basic principle of liberty in a free society where each

citizen is king and his home is his castle. Our government derives its powers from the consent of the gov-
erned. Such a system allows much latitude for the development and enjoyment of innumerable occupations
and vocations for the pursuit of happiness and national
growth. In this area of human relations the law must be
a living, breathing and informed order which knows
right from wrong; which has the courage to declare and
to protect the right, and to redress and suppress the
wrong; which conceives it to be justified only so long as
it guards with jealous care the essential liberties of free
people against oppression from any source.

"The average American citizen is scarcely aware of
what a privilege it is to live in this land of ours, pro-
tected as he is by laws which secure to him these price-
less blessings. The extent of this privilege is not ordi-
narily capable of realization until its existence is threat-
ened. In every hour of storm and stress in this land, our
law has adjusted itself to the needs of the people without sacrificing our fundamental liberties.

"The enormous development and fabulous growth
of our country reflect the wisdom and foresight of our
founding fathers in framing the Constitution of the
United States with which all the laws of the land must
harmonize. Even poverty is not a barrier here. What
greater example could be found than Abraham Lincoln, born in a log hut, but who became President of
the United States and left behind him 'footprints on
the sands of time.' His struggles and success suggests to

me a similarity to the experience and opportunity of Wake Forest and its School of Law.

"Starting without wealth or the prospect of immediate financial assistance, men of faith and courage and unselfish devotion to their country and their fellowmen fought on with unfaltering courage and inflexible faith until this law school trained more than fifty per cent of all the members of the bar in this State. They assumed their places at the bar and on the bench, in the legislative halls of the General Assembly, and of the United States Congress; they occupied the Governor's office in this and other states. Those results were accomplished with little material facilities. Dr. N. Y. Gulley and Prof. E. W. Timberlake alternated class recitations in a single room and had a scant library consisting of North Carolina Reports, U.S. Supreme Court Reports, and the American and English Encyclopedia of Law. For years the Law School was retained temporarily on the approved list of Law Schools on condition that it acquire a minimum quantity of law books for the library.

"What a change has been wrought within the last ten years! This magnificent building of brick and mortar, with numerous offices, classrooms, library facilities, and a courtroom which surpasses in beauty and utility the courtrooms of the State and Federal courts, all these combined constitute facilities of modern type and convenience unsurpassed by similar law schools in the United States.

"The judiciary of the State and Federal courts congratulate you on your wonderful achievements and express our fervent hope and confident expectation that your noble past will be but a stepping stone toward a more glorious future."

Carroll W. Weathers, Dean of the Wake Forest School of Law, also gave a wonderful talk. He summed up the sense of dedication which was felt by all who were present for the occasion:

"On this historic day we of the Law School experience two deep-felt emotions. One arises from a sense of gratitude, the other from a sense of commitment and obligation.

"There is much for which we are grateful.

"Foremost, we are grateful for the privilege of serving legal education, for the privilege of preparing young men and women for the sobering responsibilities they will assume as lawyers, and for the unlimited opportunities which will be theirs to serve society through a noble profession.

"Furthermore, we shall be mindful of those of a former era, now departed this life, that eminent triumvirate of Professors Gulley, Timberlake and White, and we are grateful for their long, dedicated and distinguished service to this School in the early years of its existence.

"But, today, we are particularly grateful for this building and the enlarged field of service it affords our School. Many have had significant part in making it possible. To these we wish to express the gratitude of the Law School:

"To President Tribble, the Administration, and the

Trustees, for authorizing the building in the initial construction program of the new College; for its superb quality, and for its adequacy;

"To the architects, Messrs. Larson and Larson, for the artistic beauty, the skillful design, and the utility of the building;

"To Basil M. Watkins, devoted alumnus, and his campaign committee, for their efforts in raising substantial funds for the building.

"To William Henley Dietrick, not a law alumnus but loyal son of Wake Forest, for his generous gift of the furniture for the administrative offices of the School;

"To the family, friends and former students of William Curtis Soule, for furnishing the Faculty Conference Room in memory of Professor Soule, valued member of our Law Faculty, whose zeal and efforts in behalf of the School never faltered;

"To Irving Carlyle and Frederick Larson for the handsome portrait of Chief Justice Marshall which adorns the wall of this Courtroom;

"To President Robert P. Burns of the Lawyer Alumni Association, and that faithful group of alumni whose material gifts have been substantial, but even more important, whose moral support, sympathetic understanding and confidence have given strength and courage to those serving the School.

"Then, I could speak at length of the cooperation, assistance and loyalty of the Law Faculty and students —and my personal gratitude to them—but they are the

Law School, and my purpose here is to speak for them and not to them.

"To all of these I wish to express the lasting gratitude of the Law School.

"On this day we feel a sobering sense of obligation to dedicate not only this building but all our resources, our energies, and our abilities to the finest traditions and highest purposes of legal education, to the noblest ideals of the legal profession. To this end . . .

"We commit the use of this building, and the purpose of this School, to the pursuit of scholarly achievement, to the maintenance of exacting standards of scholarship, to the concept that there is no easy road to excellence in legal education, but that success in the study of law as in the practice can only be achieved by hard work, conscientious application and steadfast purpose;

"We commit the use of this building not only to the improvement of legal education in our state and section, but also with our estimable neighbors, those excellent law schools at the University of North Carolina and Duke University, to the further development of an effective program of continuing legal education in our State, in collaboration with the North Carolina Bar Association;

"We commit this building and the resources of this School to the thorough training of young men and women to become competent and responsible lawyers, worthy of the confidence of clients and the commissions entrusted to their care:

"We commit the use of this building and the resources of this School, tangible and intangible, to inculcating in our students an appreciation of the ideals and purposes of the legal profession: that the objective of every lawyer in each case he tries or transaction he handles should be that justice be achieved; that no lawyer has the right to use the processes of the law to produce injustice or gain for a client that to which he is not entitled; that the purpose of the law is justice among men, and the purpose of the honorable lawyer is to seek and do justice;

"We commit the use of this building and this Law School to stimulating within the student an appreciation of the obligation of the lawyer to society, the recognition that his profession sets him apart as a man concerned with just relations and righteous living, that he possesses exceptional influence, and that it is not only his privilege but his duty to use his influence and position in behalf of a better social order, and to live as a worthy example to others;

"Finally, with a sense of dedication we commit this Law School to strive to afford young people who study within these walls some measure of insight into the meaning and purpose of life, to the end that their lives may be lived in the service of others and they may find the satisfaction that comes from a noble purpose, high ideals and exemplary living."

Sir Walter told me one time that Judge W. C. Harris, one of North Carolina's beloved Superior Court judges, told him that I had done North Carolina a great service and especially the lawyers, and that the lawyers owed to me a great debt of gratitude.

"What have I done wrong now?" I asked.

"Judge Harris told me," said Sir Walter, "that you took a trip all down through the eastern section of North Carolina giving pre-trial expositions and that you had made a human being out of Judge Johnson J. Hayes. He says that before you made that trip with Judge Hayes, when lawyers went into his court at Greensboro, they had to go in on their all-fours, sort of creep in. But since you made that trip with him, lawyers can go into his court standing straight up, and Judge Hayes will smile and shake hands with might-nigh everybody. And sometimes, since then, he has been known to put a few on probation for making liquor, and only a few weeks ago he actually appointed a Democrat as receiver in a right substantial matter."

"Well now, Sir Walter," I replied, "that *is* nice, and it makes a man feel right reasonable portionbury. But Judge Hayes and I did have a good time on that trip. By the time we returned we had won considerable fame among the lawyers and we received some substantial nicknames. When we got back, Judge Hayes was known as Judge Johnson J. Marcus Aurelius Hayes; Mr. Stahle Lynn became known as Stahle Justinian Lynn; and as for me, they just called me Epectitus, which at least ain't too high sounding in legal circles."

Returning from this trip we had arrived in Greensboro about midnight. The hotel had only one room. I told the Judge that if he didn't mind my snoring, we could get along with just one room O. K. He said, "Seawell, that won't bother me. We'll just use the same room."

So that night we retired and the Judge got in bed first. When he turned over on his back he opened up his blower and in about three hours a Diesel train passed and drowned him out a little and I finally got some sleep.

Next morning, the Judge popped out of bed early and was down in the dining room reading the paper when I got down for breakfast. "Seawell, you didn't bother me at all last night," he said.

"I guess that's right. I didn't get a chance."

"I didn't snore, did I?"

"No, but you drowned out a couple down the hall that were snorin' pretty good. But Judge, the thing that bothered me most was not your snoring but your talking in your sleep."

"Now Seawell, I didn't talk in my sleep, did I?"

"You sure did!"

"What did I say?"

"I couldn't exactly understand the first part of it but you always ended up with 'A year and a day.' "

"Pshaw," said Judge Hayes, "that is just another big lie you have made up on me."

CALL YOUR NEXT CASE.

9

SIR WALTER taught school in North Carolina in that great section of Moore, near Chatham, known as the Putnam Section. One of his first pupils was Mrs. Gilbert Muse McCaskill, wife of John McCaskill. This lady was the real foundation stone of the hospital at High Point. Sir Walter also taught Mrs. Carrie Alston, wife of Lacy Alston, the art of becoming a court reporter, and she became one of the best in the state.

The finest thing about teaching is that it makes you your own best pupil. Sir Walter learned human nature and the ways of man, which are entertaining and interesting, and sometimes also disgusting. One time while getting ready to try a case in Asheboro, the trial judge asked Sir Walter if he was ready for trial. "Yes, I'm ready Your Honor," he replied, "and I think the other side is ready. But if we try this case, I am afraid that all we do here today will be held to be null and void by the Supreme Court of the United States."

The judge, rather wild-eyed, asked why, and Sir Walter replied: "If it please the Court, there is not a single Colored person in the courtroom."

During this same term of court a trial was started and the solicitor had completed his examination of the jury and tendered them to Judge Walter. Looking over the jury for a few minutes and waiting until the courtroom was very quiet, Sir Walter asked one question. "Is there any member of this jury who goes by the name of 'Bud?' If so, let that fact be known please, and excuse yourself."

No one moved. "Your Honor, the defendant is content," said Sir Walter. The judge thought a moment and then called Sir Walter up to the bench.

"Why did you ask that question, whether or not any juror went by the name of 'Bud'?"

"Your Honor," replied Sir Walter, "in every community there is a man who goes by the name of 'Bud'. He is known to everybody as 'Bud'. He is usually an expert at everything and ain't worth a damn for nothin'. If twelve jurors have one of them named 'Bud,' it will always cause a mis-trial. If eleven were for acquittal, 'Bud' would be for conviction. 'Bud' lives in every section of North Carolina. When some one gets married, he is always the first one to go down and decorate the church. He is a good hand to take up collections, and every now and then he will elope with some member of the choir.

"When anybody dies in the community, Bud will go down to the house and stand by the coffin in the midst of the flowers, and when a pretty good crowd gets into the room, he will fold his hands one on top of the other like a new undertaker. Then when everything gets right still he will look over in the coffin and in a very melancholy voice say out loud, *'don't he look natchul'.* 'Bud' is a good fellow, all right, judge, but I just don't want him serving on any of my juries."

Sir Walter seemed to be quite serious about this "Bud" business. When a jury would come in and decide a case contrary to what Sir Walter thought it ought to be, he'd say, "They ain't got no more sense than Bud." He'd say it just like that, though he knew his English all right and could use it as beautiful as the King ever got up. But sometimes, to help show his utter disgust at something he would use to great advantage a good old two negative colloquialism, and he didn't make no apology for it neither.

One of the beautiful things about practicing law with Sir Walter was that he knew where to tap. Sir Walter, like me, never did charge enough for his "tapping," but after all, the joy of practicing law is not in how much money you can make. Of course, though money can't buy happiness, it can move you a long ways from misery. While a lot of lawyers are constantly complaining about the pitfalls of the profession, Sir Walter and I enjoyed to the uttermost the joys of the jurisdiction. Many times we were very poor in fees but we were rich with jurisprudence. Knowing where to tap is always worth more than money and there is more satisfaction in it.

Sir Walter had a serious case at Fayetteville and he wanted to continue it, but the judge had decided otherwise and stated that the case could not be continued. I asked Sir Walter what he would do and he told me that he had not fully exhausted his remedies. He wanted the court to get started and operate about a half day before he made his motion. So the first thing after lunch Sir Walter pointed out to the court that all the court had done up to the present time was null and void for the reason that the court had not put up the United States flag and the flag of the great State of North Carolina. This threw the Court into a dither, but it got the case continued, and now when you go into a courthouse in North Carolina you will see the judge sitting up between the United States flag and the flag of the great State of North Carolina.

Speaking of knowing where to tap, Sir Walter said that in all criminal cases the first thing a lawyer ought to do, is move to quash the bill of indictment, whether he has seen the bill or not. He said that about half the time it would work because most bills were drawn in a hurry and drawn wrong.

Judge Harris was on the bench at Pittsboro one day and asked Sir Walter if he were ready for trial. He said, "No, Your Honor, I am moving to quash the bill of indictment."

"What is wrong with it?"

"I haven't seen it, but I feel certain there is something wrong with it."

"Mr. Solicitor," said Judge Harris, "let me see the bill." After looking at it for about a minute, he said, "Motion allowed."

"Thank you, Your Honor," said Sir Walter. "I *felt* like something was wrong with it."

Sir Walter usually had the answer no matter who asked him the question. Arguing a case one day in the Supreme Court of North Carolina, he was attempting to show to the court the unjust matters involved, and how badly his client was being treated. Finally Chief Justice Stacy interrupted him to say: "Judge Siler, do you have any cases you can cite in support of your contentions?"

Quick as a flash Sir Walter said, "Yes, Your Honor. *In Re* Pontius Pilate, Matthew 26."

One time after arguing before the Supreme Court at some length about what had been done wrong in the trial of a case that came up from Pittsboro, Sir Walter was interrupted by a member of the court. "Judge Siler," he said, "you have told us at some length about what they did wrong in this case. Did they do *anything* right in the case when it was tried at Pittsboro?"

"Yes, Your Honor, they did," he replied earnestly. "They rang the courthouse bell without error."

Abraham Lincoln said that a lawyer's advice was his stock in trade. Sir Walter had a large inventory.

CALL YOUR NEXT CASE.

Judge Walter D. Siler

H. F. Seawell, Jr.

Above, "Where's Chub Seawell?" An amusing incident during an Eisenhower speech at Charlotte, North Carolina. Candidate Seawell makes his presence known at right. *Below,* "Chub" Seawell and "Ike" Eisenhower during 1952 campaign in North Carolina.

The Judiciary enjoys an outing. North Carolina jurists in this old photo include, left to right in foreground, Chief Justice M. V. Barnhill; Chief Justice W. A. Devin; Justice A. A. F. Seawell; J. C. Pittman, attorney; Justice Heriot Clarkson; Justice Michael Schenck, and Chief Justice J. W. Winborne.

The Honorable Susie Sharp, North Carolina's only woman judge. Photo, taken at Carthage, N. C., also shows portrait of Justice W. J. Adams.

Above, Judge F. Don Phillips at the Nurnberg War Crimes Trials.
Below, Pronouncing judgment in the trial of one of Germany's war criminals.

Above, members of the Moore County Bar and guests. In front row, left to right, Judge F. Don Phillips of Superior Court; Justice Hunt Parker of the North Carolina Supreme Court; Judge Allen Gwyn, of Superior Court. H. F. Seawell, Jr., holds the gavel, at right. *Below,* another group photo of the Moore County Bar.

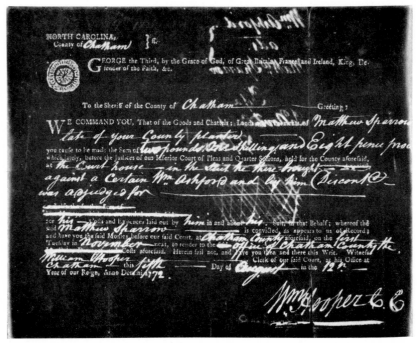

An execution issued in the name of King George the Third and signed William Hooper of Chatham County, North Carolina. Lemuel R. Johnson, Register of Deeds, found the 1772 document among old papers at the Pittsboro Courthouse. William Hooper was a signer of the Declaration of Independence.

10

SIR WALTER met me one morning between the two big columns of the courthouse in Sanford. "Good morning, My Lord," he said. "It is pleasant indeed to meet you here this beautiful morning. But I regret to report that the Crown Counsel has not yet arrived to prosecute the docket."

"Well," I said, "I am not as much interested in the Crown Counsel as I am in this young new judge who has just come upon the bench. How do you like him?"

Puffing away on his cigar and flopping his elbows like an old pelican, Sir Walter replied: "He is indeed a splendid gentleman, very affable, kind, and gracious. But I have made some personal observation, and I believe that if he was indicted for knowing the law the grand jury would return 'Not a true bill.' "

After a good laugh, I said, "Well, Brother Siler, I thought you would most likely be in court in Pittsboro this morning since they also have a term of court going on up there."

"Oh," he said, "I got my cases up in Pittsboro continued, so I could come down here. As soon as court opens here, I am going to move to continue my cases down here, so I can go back to Pittsboro."

Most of the lawyers in the state loved Judge Siler and those who didn't love him at least enjoyed him, and he was in constant demand to speak at bar meetings all over the state. Once he was asked to speak at the meeting of the bar of the Fourth Judicial District. Thanks to Mrs. Carrie Alston, court reporter from Pittsboro, part of his speech has been saved and given to me. It was in defense of the groundhog, one of Sir Walter's favorite subjects. It went like this:

"Mr. Chairman, Attorney General McMullan, fellow barristers, and all such gentlemen who do not come within the purview of any of these classifications: Please remit me the gracious privilege of saying that it always affords me unalloyed joy to meet and foregather with that group of most splendid gentlemen comprising the bar of the Fourth Judicial District.

"In stately phrase, history tells us that Thermopolae had its messenger of defeat, but the Alamo had none. Verily, Groundhog Day is the Alamo of sacred days upon the calendar. The legal profession has ever been noted for its generosity as well as its patriotism. To the cry of the oppressed, the unfortunate, and the helpless, its ear has always been attuned. In the defense of Groundhog Day we have a worthy cause and let us, en masse, rush to the rescue. The groundhog himself is in every way worthy of our most unstinted and energetic support. Before Hammurabi had placed on sale Michie's Code of Babylon; before Solon and Lycurgus had received proofs from the printers of their renowned Digests; before Cadmus had carried letters in Greece, or St. Patrick had driven snakes from Ireland, the humble groundhog was predicting weather changes with complete accuracy.

"Let us contemplate, if we can, the vast benefit that the groundhog has conferred upon agriculture. We see how seed time and harvest, and cultivation itself, wait for an expression of opinion from the friend of those who tickle the soil. Commerce and travel, football and picnics, revival meetings and prize fights, summer vacations and sleigh rides, political primaries and church conferences, firemen's tournaments and family reunions, county fairs and bridge parties, Negro festibuls and Klan konclaves, temperance rallies and the manufacture of illicit liquor, in fact everything in nature that is in any way affected by or dependent upon the weather, is most vitally interested in the integrity, the accuracy, and the dependability of the groundhog.

"The cause of the groundhog is just and we should feel proud to have a client of such high character, social prominence, and general utility. Had the mighty Napoleon consulted the groundhog instead of the French Savants, he would have known that his cannon could not have moved fast enough across the muddy fields. The battle of Waterloo would have been delayed and perhaps the whole map of Europe changed. Hitler would never have risen any higher than a house painter. The groundhog has not been treated right. We have spent thousands of dollars on the myriads of the alphabetical agencies of the New Deal—money for every conceivable purpose under the sun—but not even a marker has been erected to the humble groundhog. No congressional committee making myriads of investigations has even attempted to gather testimony as to his worthy services. No wage and hour law protects him. Old age assistance and unemployment insurance alike are denied him. The unjust treatment he has received calls for our most robust resentment and I beseech you one and all to take a firm stand for the faith. Determine in your heart that Groundhog Day shall remain unchanged forever, let come what may.

"I offer this resolution, that we covenant with each other, that we will support no man for office, accept no man as a juror, introduce no one as a witness, and represent no one as a client who is not thoroughly committed to the eternal preservation of Groundhog Day. If there be North Carolinians who would change this day and make it movable, like Easter, a firemen's fish fry, or a candidate's barbecue, let us paraphrase the eloquent outburst of Sergeant Prentice and say, 'Do this vile thing if you will, but when you do, pluck from Old Glory the star that shines for the Old North State, but leave the stripe a fit emblem of her degredation.'"

Sir Walter was a contemporary of one of the grandest gentlemen who ever graced the Bar of North Carolina, J. McN. Johnson, father of J. Talbot Johnson, who at the time of this writing is president of the Moore County Bar. Col. J. McN. had a magnificent sense of humor in the genuine Bobby Burns style. Back in the days of prohibition and B. N. D. (Before New Deal) a young man in Pinehurst by the name of Jack Latting made some most excellent wine from fruit grown on his place. But one day some prohibition agents got "wind" of it, and so they seized about a barrel of Captain Jack Latting's very fine wine. Lawyers were summoned from all quarters. Bob Lawrance from Lumberton, and Judge Varser, U. L. Spence, my father, and many others too numerous to mention.

The Recorder, Judge George Hiram Humber, was a special friend of J. McN. Johnson, who very affectionately called him "Geordie." After about a day of wrangling over the law, Judge Humber finally handed down his decision and found Captain Jack guilty and ordered the wine poured into the sewer in front of the courthouse at Carthage. The opinion didn't set so well with

Col. J. McN., so he wrote a little poem that went like this:

> Our Geordie of the dread wool sack
> Dressed out in the legal ermine
> To hear him speel the law, good lack,
> 'Twas better than a sermon.
>
> 'Twas good to hear him speel the law
> And good to hear him utter
> But he poured Jack Latting's noble wine
> In that damn nasty gutter.

CALL YOUR NEXT CASE.

11

SIR WALTER SILER and Senator Furnifold M. Simmons were built on the same last. They had about the same wheelbase, sort of like a big, strong, two-horse wagon with a short couplin' pole. Back in the twenties Sir Walter was one of the electors-at-large in a presidential election and he and Senator Furnifold M. had their pictures "tuck" while delivering the North Carolina vote in the canvass meeting at Washington. They made quite a picture together and it is a pity that such a picture could not be preserved for posterity because you could tell by looking at the picture that here was a couple of unusual men, both of them experts in their fields, with two yellows in their heads.

It is doubtful if any man will ever live again in North Carolina who will control the political situation from the palm of his hand like Senator Simmons. He was for North Carolina—first, last, and all the time. He was the soul of honor and integrity, and he gave the Republicans constant hell and harassment until 1928 when he jumped in and carried the state for Hoover against what he called a group of liberal imposters.

Sir Walter and Senator Simmons both were as strong in their political beliefs as is possible for men to be, but Sir Walter knew that no matter which side was elected, it was very doubtful if the millienium would be ushered in and the Lord decide to move in with us in order to be more comfortable.

One day Sir Walter and I were talking about honest men running for public office. He said that when he picked up the paper and read all the political advertisements he was utterly amazed at the great number of the "People's Choices" who had themselves so advertised. Sitting over at Mount Vernon Springs one day we decided to sort of analyze the situation and just see what a real honest man would say about himself when he offered himself for public office. "Now please bear in mind that we are talking about a truly-solid-honest man, not a semi-honest man nor a quasi-honest man, but a real-completely-honest man," said Sir Walter. If such a man should ever run for office, we decided he would put his campaign advertisements in the paper like this, and there would be ten cardinal points he would use:

1.

I AM NOT THE PEOPLES CHOICE; I AM MY OWN CHOICE. Now that kind of statement would have a considerable element of truth in it and could be relied upon to be bordering on the truth.

2.

MY FRIENDS DID NOT URGE ME TO RUN FOR OFFICE. THEY HAD BETTER SENSE. I DID IT OF MY OWN FREE WILL AND ACCORD. How many times have we seen where some candidate puts an ad in the paper saying that his friends had urged him to run for office. What a terrible reflection on his friends.

3.

I AM NOT QUALIFIED AND HAVE HAD NO EXPERIENCE BUT BELIEVE I CAN MAKE AS BIG A MESS OF IT AS ANY ONE RUNNING. Sir Walter and I agreed that here was one statement that would be hard for even an honest man to make. Most newspaper ads gotten up by a candidate brag at considerable length on the qualifications and experience of the candidate, gotten up by the candidate for the candidate.

4.

I CAN BE BOUGHT IF THE PRICE IS RIGHT. This golden truth has never before been published— not in the annals of recorded history—not from the time Lot ran for Mayor of Sodom even down to this present periodical perpendicular.

5.

MY LIFE IS NOT AN OPEN BOOK. IF IT WERE, I WOULD MOST LIKELY BE RUN OUT OF THE COUNTY. Sir Walter and I agreed that one of the biggest lies published in the history of politics is that old familiar one that you see in most all papers when campaigns are held for public office: "My life is an open book in this community." There never has been any man whose life was an open book in any place he ever lived. We both agreed also that if our lives and all we had ever done or said were an open book, we would want to tear out a multitude of pages and close said book. If there was any truth at all in such matters, and every person's life was an open book, and all he ever said or did in public or private was revealed, millions would cry for the rocks and hills to fall on them and hide them from the face of such a book. *The whole world stands guilty before God that no flesh should glory in His presence. The wages of sin is death, and the strength of sin is the law, but thanks be to God who giveth us the victory through Jesus Christ our Lord.* Sir Walter and I agreed that hell was overflowing with self-righteous folks who claimed their lives to be an open book, when they were really in rebellion against God and in sin and they had refused to accept Christ as personal savior.

6.

MY FRIENDS DID NOT PAY FOR THIS AD. I PAID FOR IT MYSELF, AND THEY AGREED THAT I MIGHT PUT SUCH A STATEMENT IN THE PAPER. This is one that you most always see. Some candidate is always putting an ad in the paper and stating that same was paid for by his friends. This sounds good to the unsuspecting and looks good to the candidate, but most times there is no truth in it.

7.

IF ELECTED I PROMISE TO RUN THE OFFICE ABOUT LIKE I PLEASE AND TO SUIT MYSELF, UNTIL JUST BEFORE ELECTION TIME, AT WHICH TIME I WILL BEGIN TO BE FRIENDLY AND START SPEAKING TO EVERBODY AND SHAKING HANDS. This is the statement of an honest man. How many votes could he get if he put that in the paper? Yet it is the true pattern of most office holders.

8.

I HAVE NOT BEEN A LIFELONG DEMOCRAT (OR REPUBLICAN). I HAVE OFTEN VOTED

FOR THE MAN IN THE OTHER PARTY AND
KEPT MY MOUTH SHUT. When a man advertises
that he is the kind of man that has never split his ticket,
it is most likely untrue, but if it is true, he usually isn't
worth voting for, as he is only advertising his own nar-
row mind.

9.

IF ELECTED I WILL TAKE A FIRM NEUTRAL
STAND ON ALL CONTROVERSIAL MATTERS
AND WILL DO ALL I CAN TO STAY IN OFFICE
AS LONG AS I LIVE. This is most likely the very
mudsill of all political truth, especially among Con-
gressmen. After a politician once gets into office, a firm
neutral stand is often hard to beat.

10.

I WISH TO THANK ALL MY FRIENDS FOR
THEIR SUPPORT. BUT PLEASE DON'T COME
HANGING AROUND ME WANTING FAVORS
OR TRYING TO BORROW MONEY. I'LL BE
SEEING YOU IN FOUR YEARS. A "thank you"
notice like that would be honest and true as to nearly
all candidates who ever ran for office, and Sir Walter
and I agreed that as far as we could ascertain, no truly-
solid-honest man or woman had ever run for office in
this or any other State. We decided that if old Diogenes
(who went around with a lantern in the daytime looking for an honest man) had lived in our day, he would

have run out of oil long before Roosevelt, the New Dealer, was elected.

Justice Carlyle Higgins, of the North Carolina Supreme Court, the old Sage of Sparta, the old Blue Beard of the Blue Ridge, and one of the finest North Carolinians that ever lived, told me that back when the country voted for Harding and "normalcy" an old mountaineer came down out of the high mountains to Sparta and in a short while got reasonable drunk and decided to put on a one-man celebration. So he took his shotgun and paraded down the street at Sparta and announced that none but Republicans could cross the street. He marched with his shotgun on his shoulder from one end of the street to the other, and halted everyone who passed, and inquired whether they were Republican or Democrat, announcing that no one but a Republican would be permitted to pass. He would bring his gun down in a threatening manner and cry "Halt! Are you a Republican or a Democrat? None but Republicans are allowed to pass here today. No Democrats allowed."

Justice Higgins said that he had to cross the street to go from his office over to the courthouse, and that he was hoping not to have any trouble with the old man. He put his papers in one pocket and an owlhead pistol in the other, and waited until the old man had gotten to the other end of the street, and he started across. But just about the time he reached the middle of the street, the old man spied him. Whirling around, and bringing the gun down in a very threatening manner, the old man ordered him to halt. Justice Higgins said he stood still until the old man got up close to him. Then the old man looked him right close in the eye and said, "Are you a Democrat or a Republican?"

Justice Higgins replied, "Well, I will have to be honest about this thing. I am a Democrat."

The old man threw down his gun and grabbed Justice Higgins by the hand and began to shake it. "Brother," he declared, "I'm shore pleased to meet you. You know, the Democrats have been damn scarce around here all day."

CALL YOUR NEXT CASE.

12

SIR WALTER and satire went together like Hoover and the Depression, hand in hand. He did not mean any harm by it. It just came sort of natural. He told me that in the summertime Goldsboro was in the same relation to hell as Brooklyn was to New York —next door. Which is a sort of round-about way of telling how hot Goldsboro is in the good old summertime.

When I think of Goldsboro I think of the time Judge Clawson Williams (who never took a drink of liquor in his life), charged the jury in court at Goldsboro on a drunk-driving case. He said: "Now gentlemen of the jury, the great danger about driving drunk, or under the influence, is that a man thinks he is over here when he is really over yonder. And when he thinks he is over yonder he is really over here. It is dangerous because a man isn't sure just where he is when he is under the influence."

He sort of hesitated a little and about that time an old man whispered out loud to another old man on the front row, "That judge has been drunk, all right. He knows what he is talking about."

I never think of Goldsboro that I don't think of the time that my grandfather, Dr. V. N. Seawell, was in Mr. Weil's store when two old codgers came in, one a hunchback and the other one bowlegged. The hunchback spoke up and said, "Mr. Weil, I want to get a hump-back coat for myself and a pair of bowlegged britches for my friend."

My father said that one time he was walking down the street in Goldsboro and met an old colored man, who asked him if he wasn't the son of Dr. V. N. Seawell. He told him he was and the colored man said: "Lawd have mercy! Dr. Seawell was the best doctor I ever knowed. He was truly a fine doctor; he doctored my wife when she died."

It was in Goldsboro in the year 1922 when the University of North Carolina defeated Wake Forest College to the tune of 63 to 3, but it was the best thing that ever happened to the Baptists. It aroused some kind of sleeping, worldly ambition in their souls and they continued to grow in works until they have finally pitched their tent, like Lot of old, towards Winston-Sodom. It wouldn't be right to ask if any good thing can come out of Goldsboro, because it was here that the Baptists got Baptized with fire one day and got started over again. Goldsboro was the same thing to the Baptists as Gideon was to the Three Hundred.

Some of North Carolina's finest citizens live in Goldsboro and it is one of North Carolina's finest towns, but my grandfather said he remembered Goldsboro when it only had thirteen stores and all *fourteen* of them were bar rooms. And he told about the time Cousin John and Cousin Bill went down to Goldsboro and traded at every store. The story also reminds me of Governor Scott, who introduced the famous slogan, "Going forward with Scott" and who also raised the windows at Raleigh and let in a little fresh air. Some said it wasn't so fresh, but at least it was a change.

My grandfather said that Cousin John and Cousin Bill went down to Goldsboro driving old Nellie to a little road cart, and that from about four o'clock in the P. M. until about ten, they visited all the bars and got reasonably drunk and started home. Old Nellie hadn't taken anything and she followed the old sandy winding road down through the woods, picking her way along in the dark. A tree had fallen down across the road, and Nellie crossed over the trunk and stopped with her heels just over the log, and the log between her heels and the wheels of the cart. Not knowing what was wrong, Bill asked, "Cousin John, can't you get her to go forward?"

"I don't know," John replied.

"Cluck to her a little."

John clucked a little, and old Nellie just shivered in the harness and stood still. "Now look-a-here Cousin John," said Bill. "We got to go forward. Have you got airy buggy whup, tap her up a little."

John tapped her up a little but old Nellie just shook in the harness and wouldn't move. Finally, Bill got impatient. "Now look-a-here Cousin John, we got to go forward. Shower down on her." So John showered down with the whip and old Nellie jerked out of the harness and the cart went over backwards and left John and Bill lying in the old sandy road.

Bill, feeling around in the dark, called out: "John, air you hurt?"

"No, Bill. Air you hurt?"

"No, I ain't hurt. But Cousin John, I just got one remark I want to make. You may not be able to get her to go forward, but damn if you can't back her up faster than anyone I ever seed."

One time the North Carolina Bar Association took a cruise. We went up to Nova Scotia. We thought we would escape the heat. When we landed at the dock at Halifax a newsboy was hollerin' EXTRA. We threw over a shillin' and got a paper and the headlines said, "30 Die In Heat Wave In Halifax." We went from Halifax (which we changed to Helifax), fifty miles to Grand Pre, via a train somewhat on the order of the old wood-burning Winston-Salem Southbound. Coming back to Halifax most folks took off all the clothes they could and got barefooted. Riding down from Grand Pre it was a disgusted looking crowd. No one was saying a word. The train stopped at a little station and everything was still as death. Finally Hip Martin spoke up and said, "Children don't cry. Your pappy will buy a watermelon when we get to Goldsboro." Knowing Goldsboro, it cheered us up considerable and some even took a drink of Vichy water.

CALL YOUR NEXT CASE.

13

SIR WALTER tried cases all over North Carolina and in other states and on one occasion struck a legal gusher and went down into the great state of Texas and tried a law suit which involved about 500 plaintiffs and defendants. In selecting the jury, Sir Walter asked them only one question: "If any of you jurors think that a man from North Carolina is a Yankee just let that fact be known and excuse yourself." He said that since Texas is two hundred and sixty-five times larger than Rhode Island, there would be any number of folks in Texas who don't like to use the word

"North" under any circumstances. Like some folks in South Carolina who, when they refer to *North* Carolina, had rather not use the word "North;" so they call North Carolina *Upper* South Carolina, which is reasonable and seems to state the case.

Down in Conroe, Texas, Judge Siler represented the Strickland heirs. He told me about one lawyer appearing in the case who had come from Georgia and had been in Texas for some time. He was about to decide to run for governor. If all the clients could have moved in and voted for him, it would have given him a good lead in the race. This kind of a case just suited Sir Walter. There were from first to last 93 lawyers who appeared in it. Five thousands people were involved, including the widow of Babe Ruth, a relative of Woodrow Wilson, and also the widow of Huey Long, according to the Conroe paper.

This kind of "carryin's on" was joy to the soul of Sir Walter. Having not seen him for some time, when I asked where he had been, the said he had been stricken with "the Stricklands" and had for six months been transporting family Bible to Texas. Sir Walter said that he proved that Sam Houston, in command of a small force of Wilson Stricklands, annihilated the army of Santa Anna at Vinces Bridge on the San Jacinto River, with small loss to the Texans. Only seven Wilson Stricklands killed and 13 Wilson Stricklands wounded. There were at least 36 Wilson Stricklands in the law suit.

The New York *Sunday News* had this to say about

the case, in their issue of March 16th, 1941: "The Judge, jury and lawyers involved in this case might have long ago became candidates for the psychopathic ward had not the scene been considerably enlivened by touches of the unusual and the plain comic. Judge Walter D. Siler of Pittsboro, North Carolina, chief counsel for a block of 500 North Carolina Stricklands, has achieved the status of Court Jester. He issues a journal on the case and calls it by various names—The Strickland Sentinel — The Vince Vindicator — The Humble Hopes."

This case had been running six years before Judge Siler got into it, and I asked him some time before he passed away what happened to the case. All he would say was, "Some of the others are presenting their evidence now and I presume that there will be another crop of heirs by the time these get through. And then we can start all over again." Sir Walter maintained that the Wilson Strickland whom he claimed was the right one was the only simon-pure, double-distilled, blown-in-the-bottle Strickland, and that it was a dastardly untruth that Wilson Strickland had been run out of North Carolina because he had joined the Republican Party. According to Sir Walter, "Where there is a will, there's heirs; and where there ain't no will, there's a multitude."

Conroe, Texas, is northwest of Houston. Many jurors were farmers and most of them rented out their farms, as it appeared they would be on this case many crop years. Some of the original plaintiffs died while the trial was in progress and it was necessary to stop the trial and go into the process of appointing administrators and executors and guardians. When Sir Walter went down there with his evidence, it consisted of a stack of family Bibles that would reach almost to the ceiling of the courthouse, if piled one on top of the other. He claimed that in many were founds the letters G.T.T., which, he said, positively stood for "Gone To Texas." When Sir Walter got back from Texas he said that he did not believe in taking any post-graduate courses in Calamity Howling. His attitude was: "My days are consumed like smoke, and my bones are burned as a hearth; my heart is smitten and withered like grass, so that I forget to eat my bread. By reason of the voice of my groaning my bones cleave to my skin. I am like a pelican of the wilderness; I am like an owl of the desert. I have eaten ashes like bread and mingled my drink with weeping, *in short, I ain't going back to Texas.*"

Which brings up the proposition of a man who went to Sir Walter to get him to draw his will, and he said that he wanted to leave everything to his wife with the provision that she marry within twelve months after his death or she could not have it. When asked to explain such a peculiar request the client replied, "Well, I want to be darn sure that there will be at least one man left on earth who is genuinely sorry that I ever died."

CALL YOUR NEXT CASE.

14

SIR WALTER loved North Carolina with all his heart. He loved history and the people who went into the building of history. He loved current events and the characters responsible for current events. He enjoyed comparing old-timers with the present "nincompoots," as he often called them.

It took a man of considerable knowledge of world, local and ancient events to keep up with Sir Walter, and just such a man was His Honor William H. Sumner Burgwyn, of the North Carolina Superior Court bench. He told me one day that Judge Burgwyn was highly interested in "might-nigh" everything and everybody, and it suited him. He said he wasn't too big to be touched in the heart and shed a tear or two, and was just the right size for laughing purposes.

In my opinion, Judge Burgwyn also had a faint touch of knowledge of the Grace of God. We often discussed old preacher John Newton who wrote the very famous hymn, "Amazing Grace, how sweet the sound, that saved a wretch like me." Sir Walter said one time, that about the best way to describe Judge Burgwyn was in the vernacular of Shakespeare, that is, speaking in the flesh and not in the spirit, "He was a veritable 'Tickle-Brain'." Truly, Judge Burgwyn did enjoy a joke on himself, and like Judge Don Phillips, he seemed to enjoy it more than any one else.

Judge Burgwyn was a powerful Episcopalian. One day he journeyed over into the Commonwealth of Virginia on business for the Episcopalians and fell among thieves who stripped him of his raiment and left him wounded by the wayside. But it wasn't long before all the good Samaritans of North Carolina, even including Judge Hunt Parker, rallied and appeared on the scene and set his feet back on Zion, where they have been ever since and should never have been taken off. So it was a joyful occasion when Glenn Cobb of the Cumberland Bar, along with many other distinguished lawyers from throughout the State of North Carolina, gave a testimonial dinner for Judge Quincy A. Nimocks, Superior Court Judge, and Judge Burgwyn was named toastmaster. After Mr. Cobb had made quite a flowery introduction of Judge Burgwyn, and everyone stood to their

feet in great respect and admiration, the orchestra began to play the familiar tune, *Carry Me Back to Old
Virginny*. When the strains of the old song began, tears
flowed down the cheeks of all present, but it wasn't
because of a sad and melancholy heart. Joy was unre-
strained, and humor had reached a new zenith on the
banks of the old Cape Fear. Nobody enjoyed it more
than Judge Burgwyn, who also shed considerable tears
himself.

As for Judge Burgwyn, if your mind is not alert and
pretty quick on the trigger you'll be left wondering
what it is all about, because he is not going to explain
anything to you. If a man has to have all his humor
explained to him, he hasn't got any. Most of the judges
of the Superior Court of North Carolina are not only
learned in the law but they are what I would call classic
gentlemen. They love music and art and all the cultural
things. Judge Hoyle Sink told me though that Judge
Burgwyn was not the only judge who ever had music
played especially for him. He said that one time in
Greensboro they were having a dance at a tobacco warehouse and he knew that this ought to be a fine time to
meet many of his constituents. So he decided to go
down and look over the situation. He found a multitude of folks gathered, and about the time he came to
the big open door, it was between dances and folks had
sort of cleared the floor and were over against the four
walls of the large warehouse.

As he started to go in the door with some friends who
were with him, several people remarked "Here comes

Judge Sink." And when he reached a place where everybody in the whole warehouse could see him, the band began to play, "I'll be glad when you're dead, you rascal you." Judge Sink, with that twinkle in his steely blue eyes, and waterin' all the time, told me: "Chub, that might have been an accident, or a coincidence, but it looked mighty damn suspicious to me!" So Judge Burgwyn ain't the only one who ever had music dedicated to him even if the one for Judge Sink was an accident.

Judge Burgwyn often held court in Greensboro. At one term of criminal court a few years ago, a very prepossessing woman was seated just inside the bar. She was one of these women who sort of grip onto a man in his idea of beauty. She was one of these women who didn't exactly walk down the street, but sort of rippled down the street. If she needed any money, she would just go down to the First National Bank and withdraw the president. After court opened, Judge Burgwyn called Shelly Caviness up to the bench and asked, "What is that woman doing sitting here in the bar?"

"That is my client," replied Mr. Caviness.

"What in the world is she doing here at a criminal term of the court?"

"She has been charged with driving under the influence, Your Honor," replied Mr. Caviness, "but the officer said he just smelled a little alcohol, and thought that she was unsteady on her feet."

Judge Burgwyn said, "Well, that's too bad," and let Mr. Caviness return to his seat. Then Judge Burgwyn put on his glasses and took a good look straight at the

lady. Then he put his glasses up over his head and took a good look at her with his naked eye. He turned sideways and got a good look from an angle. He put his glasses down on the end of his nose and looked at her over the top of his glasses.

Then he called Mr. Caviness back to the bench by getting his eye and crooking his finger at him. When Mr. Caviness reached the bench, Judge Burgwyn leaned over close to him and said, "She ain't guilty."

Shelly Caviness told me that when Judge Burgwyn charged the jury he said, among other things: "Gentlemen of the jury, the officer said he smelled something like alcohol on this lady. Maybe he did, but you know that all women wear perfume, and all perfume has an alcohol base. But of course the officer said he smelled alcohol and maybe he did. He also said that this lady was unsteady on her feet. Of course women wear these high heel shoes. They're pretty, and make women look mighty pretty. All the women wear them, but because of these high heels, all women are unsteady on their feet, and especially if they get out on the road where there is a lot of gravel like the officer said it was at this place. Of course, he said she was unsteady on her feet, and maybe she was. It is a question for you, gentlemen. Take the case and see how you find."

Mr. Caviness said the jury did get the door shut just in time to open it up again and come back and report "Not Guilty." He said Judge Burgwyn then crooked his finger at him again and called him to the bench and said, 'See there, by golly. I told you so."

Judge Burgwyn once told Sir Walter about the Judge who had sentenced a man to die and then asked him if he had anything to say. Whereupon the man stood up and said, "Yes, Your Honor. It may be that a lot of folks around here have a lot of respect for Your Honor. And a lot of folks around here may look up to Your Honor. And some folks around here may love Your Honor. But you have done gone and ruint yourself with me!"

CALL YOUR NEXT CASE.

15

SIR WALTER maintained that culture and refinement did not result from education. He said that some of the most vulgar people he had ever met were very highly educated and some of the most ignorant had in them a sense of splendid good taste and good manners. He said that all the lawyers and the Bench of North Carolina, and most certainly all the Superior Court judges of this state, were men of culture and refinement.

One man in particular, he said, stood out in his mind. That was Judge Henry Grady, who once held court in

Goldsboro with two big pistols up on the judge's bench just in order to be sure that no confusion got into the proceedings. One of the best speeches ever made at any meeting of the North Carolina Bar Association was made in 1926 at the meeting of the Bar at Wrightsville Beach. Judge Grady delivered it in a wonderful manner, and as Andrew H. Brown would say, "It made an imprint on me I ain't never forgot."

One of Judge Grady's favorite stories concerned the attitude of a man by the name of Bass. He said they called him John Pond Bass because he lived out on an island in a little natural lake down in eastern North

Carolina. Judge Grady said that John Pond Bass used
to do nothing but sit on the little dock that led up to
his house where the boats landed, and whittle and
chew tobacco and cuss out the Hobbses, a family that
lived over on another little island in an adjoining lake.
Old man John Pond would cuss out the Hobbses all
week and then invite all the neighbors in for Sunday.
When a large crowd had gathered to hear the cussin',
he would really put on a Sunday afternoon of cussin'
out the Hobbses that was truly a sight to see and hear.
One summer a Methodist preached by the name of
McKelway came down close to the lake and put up a
tent and preached for about two weeks. But old man
John Pond wouldn't go out to hear him preach. One
day the preacher got a boat and rowed himself over to
where old man John Pond was sitting, walked up to
him and said: "Is this Mr. Bass?"

"Yes, Bass is my name and what mought be yourn?"

"McKelway is my name. I am a Methodist preacher.
I have been preaching over to the tent about two weeks
and I notice that you haven't been out to hear me
preach."

Old man Bass replied: "No, I hain't been and I
hain't a-gwine."

"Did you ever stop to think about your soul?" asked
the preacher.

"No, I hain't never give it no thought."

"Mr. Bass, do you ever read the Bible?"

"No," said Bass, "I hain't never read in it none. The
old lady and gals takes a spell at it now and agin, but I
hain't never read in it none."

"Mr. Bass," said preacher McKelway, "did you ever stop to think about Judgment Day?"

"It 'pears like I have heerd tell of that day. How long air it agoin' to last?"

"Mr. Bass, there won't be but one day of it."

"Then that leaves me out, Preacher. It will take God all day long to judge them damn Hobbses over yander!"

Judge Grady knew many stories and understood the attitudes and quirks of the human mind and could see what would be humorous to others. He could also tell a serious story that would bring tears to your eyes. Sometimes folks cry on purpose and at the right time to get what they want. Similarly, it is said that of 4,002 women who fainted in 1958, 4,001 of them fainted into the arms of a man; the other one was sick.

Judge Grady told about the time an old man down east died and all his folks came to the old home place. One of the boys went into the kitchen as soon as he arrived and got a big chicken drumstick for himself and was out by the side of the house eating it, when his brother came up to him. "John," said the brother, "you know that Grandpap is dead. It looks like you'd be crying instead of eatin'. Don't you know that Grandpap is dead, John?"

"Now you git from here and leave me alone," said John. "I know Grandpap is dead and when I git through eatin' this chicken bone I'm gonna cry like hell."

Sir Walter said one time that this country would have already perished out and been forgotten if it had not been for hot dogs and hamburgers, and all politics would have long ceased if it hadn't been for barbecue. In fact, he said that the only way the Republicans could get anyone to come out to a rally in 1932 was to promise to feed the crowd. And in fact, the thing got so badly out of hand that instead of having an election in 1936, we had a sale. Which brings to mind another story of Judge Grady about the barbecue that was held in a little schoolyard down east during a hot political campaign. Some obstreperous fellow kept making everybody uncomfortable, and finally a fellow named Bill got tired of his talk and tangled with him in a fist fight. There was a township constable present who was in favor of Bill giving the fellow a lickin'. An old rail fence ran through the grounds where the barbecue was being held and it was the dividing line of the township.

The Constable got up on the first rail and demanded peace, but they kept on fighting. So he climbed up on the second rail and in the name of law demanded peace, but they kept on fighting. Finally he got up on top of the fence, and in a loud voice, in the name of God and Country, demanded that the fighting cease. But about the time he finished saying his demands the old top rail broke and threw him and he fell over in the other township. As he was getting up and brushing himself off he said, "Give him hell, Bill. This old top rail busted and throwed me outen my jurisdiction."

Judge Grady was one of the most distinguished men North Carolina ever produced. With his splendid head of white hair and his flashing blue eyes, he made quite a picture when he went walking, swinging his gold headed cane. It brings back thoughts of the time that someone asked the old colored man who was the best judge that held court at a certain place. "I been attending this here court many long years," he said. "I have done seen judges come and judges go, and who is the best and who is the smartest I can't right reasonably tell. But I is positive of one thing of which I is shore, and that is that Judge Henry Grady do appear to have more *jurisdiction* than all the rest."

CALL YOUR NEXT CASE.

16

SIR WALTER loved everybody and everything connected with Chatham County, including High Sheriff John Emmerson and his Chief Deputy, Lacy (The Democrat) Johnson. Chatham County has had some very distinguished officers and to name them all would be impossible. They have even had a Republican sheriff, the mother of the distinguished Lawyer Thompson, at present junior law partner of that sterling Presbyterian, Wade Barber. Barber was at one time a law partner of Sir Walter Siler.

When the distinguished law firm of Siler & Barber tangled with the distinguished firm of Horton & Bell with a few others thrown in for good measure, the ground was pretty well tore up from the battle, and you could hear leaves and trash still falling several days after court had adjourned. This was especially true if the old Republican, L. P. Dixon, got into the tanglement and was given a sort of a free hand, summoning up a few of the Paschals, who were pretty well mixed up politically, to sort of call signals and run interference.

Sir Walter loved all the lawyers and all the office holders in Chatham and he especially loved the history of famous folks who had lived in Chatham. His successor on the bench, Judge J. L. Moody, is a true successor of Sir Walter, because he often remarks that he does not permit some one else to run his court. Judge Moody, like Sir Walter, has a mind of his own. He is also the soul of honesty and integrity and doesn't waste time with trifling things. He hits the nail on the head and goes on to something else, and leans all the time on the side of mercy and common sense.

Sir Walter said that John Emmerson was one of the finest and smartest sheriffs Chatham County ever had. Emmerson loves to catch all kinds of criminals and he does it with dispatch. Murderers, bank robbers, house breakers, and thieves, are quickly apprehended. But if you want a man caught *instantaneously*, just let him appear in Chatham County with a pint of liquor—tax paid or non-tax paid. Sir Walter said that John Emmerson was the only sheriff he ever knew who was constantly committing ambush upon himself. He said that

Sheriff John, so he understood, owned a considerable block of stock in the company that makes Bromo-Seltzer and that one of the main things that went hand in hand with all kinds of liquor, stump hole or store bought, was Bromo-Seltzer, that old head restorer. Therefore, every time Sheriff Emmerson raided a still or made a capture he was just committing ambush on himself, unbeknowst to himself.

Sir Walter said one time that speaking of paradoxes, one of the most beautiful ones he ever saw was a big man playing a drum and leading a prohibition parade, chewing cloves.

Sir Walter was proud of Chatham because in it lived a man named William Hooper who was one of the signers of the Declaration of Independence. Elsewhere in this book is a reproduction of an execution issued by him in the name of King George III. William Hooper was the first clerk of court in Chatham and Sir Walter took me into the courthouse and showed to me some of his signings, beginning with the year 1771. It is interesting to note that in the writ of execution signed by him in 1772, he is ordering something paid in the name of the King of England, "herein fail not at your peril etc," but just a short while later he put his hand to the Declaration of Independence, wherein it was stated that King George and his cohorts were practicing tyranny on the people and that the king had sent hordes of agents to spy out the substance of the people of the colonies and that they were wrongfully seizing the property of the people and burdening them with taxes unjust and impossible to pay; that these agents of the king were flooding the country and no man was safe in his papers and property. Sir Walter said that the only difference now is that we have shifted such activities from George III over to the Treasury Department, and government agents are now eating us out of house and home, and a man isn't any more safe now in his property and papers than he was under George III, if the government claims you owe them anything.

"Of course," said Sir Walter, "we all owe something because we have determined to buy friendship all over the world and pay cash for it. We are still the land of the brave, but the home of the free may be sold for taxes. We have all gone what might be called 'internationally crazy.' If a main isn't in favor of some form of international government, or world system of government, he is said to be a narrow-minded, vulgar, provincial nationalist. In other words when we sing, 'My country 'tis of thee, sweet land of liberty,' we are just vulgar, narrow-minded, provincial nationalists. Imagine such a condition."

After discussing this matter at some length Sir Walter and I decided that in order to be up with the times we should re-write, "My country 'tis of thee" and bring it up to date. A lot of folks like Mrs. Eleanor Roosevelt, Gen. George Marshall, Secretary of State Dulles and even President Ike might be embarrassed to sing such an old-fashioned song. Who wants to be considered a vulgar, narrow-minded, provincial nationalist? We don't want any more Declarations of Independence. What we want is a Declaration of Utter Dependence. So in desperation we decided that it was our patriotic, international duty to re-write at least one verse of *America* so we would be truly liberal and progressive and world-minded. We thought one time we would get Congressman Cooley or Congressman Deane to put a bill through Congress to change this verse and bring it up to the times, but Mr. Cooley was in India studying farm conditions over there and Mr. Deane was bogged down in Switzerland knee deep in moral rearmament. So we just decided to file our verse in the archives. This is it and whether we like it or not it's mostly true and seems to state the case.

"AMERICA"
(Re-wrote for the Liberals)

My world 'tis of Thee
Sweet globe of every nationalitee,
Of thee we have decided to sing.
Long may our internationalism be bright
With a loan for every known parasite
From every farm and home and factory site
LET TAXATION RING.

Now there is nothing provincial about a verse like that and the very first words really take in the territory. Imagine singing "God Bless America" when you can sing a verse like that one which takes in the whole wide world.

Sir Walter said that if Cornwallis could come back to America there would still be a place he could recognize and that was Pittsboro, the County Seat of Chatham. He would also feel right much at home, for if he would look in the office of the Register of Deeds, he could find a number of old papers issued in the name of George III, under whom he was operating when he put up at the old Exline Hotel. Which reminds me of what Mrs. Exline said about voting for Hoover. She said she voted for him in 1928 and she was going to vote for him again in 1932 and prove to the old scoundrel that he couldn't starve her out of Pittsboro. Which gives a good picture of the kind of real quality in character and determination that exists in the Great State of Chatham. No wonder they produced a signer of the Declaration of Independence, even if a short time prior thereto he was issuing writs of seizure in the name of George II. Mr. L. R. Johnson, the present register of deeds in Chatham is the man who found this writ issued by William Hooper and gave a copy to me. Like many Chatham folks he realizes that as time marches on, people forget some of the great men of Chatham.

Judge Burgwyn asked the grand jury in Chatham one day if any of them knew a famous man named Lane who was one of the leaders of Chatham. No one could answer. He then asked if they knew for whom Chatham County was named, and if they knew where the name Pittsboro came from. No one could answer.

Tom Sawyer was asked one time to name two of the

disciples and he said David and Goliath, which was scandalously wrong but at least it was a try.

Which brings up the story about the teacher who told all the young folks to put away their books as she was going to give a little test. Starting down the front row with a little boy about nine years old she asked, "Who signed the Declaration of Independence?" The little boy looked up at her and began to whimper and a little tear flowed down his cheek and he looked up at the teacher and said, "Damn it, I never signed it." Whereupon the teacher said, "What in the world do you mean speaking out like that? You go home at once. Using such language! Here, take this note to your father."

The little boy took the note home and the father carried him away around behind the kitchen stove and sat him down in an old cane-bottomed chair and said, "Boy, I have always taught you that honesty was always the best policy. Now if you did sign it, just go ahead and say so."

CALL YOUR NEXT CASE.

17

SIR WALTER said to me one day, "Nobody has ever been born into the world who understood women, not even a woman. About the only thing that a man of good common sense understands about women is that he doesn't understand them." This kind of a statement is a most wonderful statement and is good for the soul.

The saddest thing that can ever happen to a man is for him to get the idea that he is a devil with the women. Sir Walter used to say that man born of a woman is of but few days and full of arthritis for he cometh forth in the morning like a grasshopper and is cut down in the evening like a jackass.

North Carolina had a woman sheriff before it ever had a woman judge. Miss Myrtle Siler (later Mrs. Thompson, mother of The Honorable Reid Thompson, Attorney, of Pittsboro) was Sheriff of Chatham County back in the roaring twenties. Of course, the first woman judge we had here in North Carolina was Miss Susie Sharp. She practiced right much before she went on the bench, and in arguing a case before the Supreme Court down in Raleigh, she began to address the Court by saying, "This case was tried by Judge A. M. Stack, but there are other errors set forth in the record."

I asked Judge Siler one day what he thought of a woman judge and he said, "Well, I guess it is all right, but it just runs crossways of my thoughts on jurisprudence." He said one time that a man came to him to appear in a matter and he asked what he wanted and he said, "I don't want nuthin' but a continuance of my case. I just can't go to court before no woman judge. I want my case continued. I been married 25 years and my wife can smell beer over the telephone and I done and had considerable experience with women. A woman has got a thing about her that they call a woman's ignition and when she gets that thing tuned in right, she can find out more about a man accidently than a man can find out on purpose. I got to have my case continued. If I go up there before that woman judge, she'll cross me up shore as hell and might hang me on the back side of the court room. Judge Siler, if you had been drove hard and put up muddy like me, you wouldn't want to go up agin' no woman judge. God knows, I'd rather be tried by Pontius Pilate or even Judge Hunt Parker."

Judge Susie Sharp put quite considerable fear into the lawyers and the defendants when she first went on the bench, but this was only the natural fear that gets into a man when he begins to have to deal with a woman who is taking a man's place. When Miss Susie first went on the bench a very difficult matter arose and one of the Superior Court judges very graciously offered to exchange courts so that she would not have to try a certain matter. But Miss Susie said that she took the job with her eyes wide open and she would try whatever came to hand. She is not only a very charming and gracious lady, but has made a splendid judge of the North Carolina Superior Court.

Sir Walter said that he guessed that women had been in the law business a long time, and that maybe the first woman lawyer was a young woman named Salome. He said that he understood that her motions before the court met with great approval.

Of course, if men quit running after women and women quit running after men, there would be no human race, which of course is a reasonable deduction and seems to state the case. Sometimes when you make a statement like that you have to wait and give people a little time to catch what you said. It is like saying that women add form to any occasion. Which reminds me of the old colored preacher down in Southern Pines, who preached on "Form" one time. His sermon went something like this:

"In the beginning God created the heavens and the earth, and the earth was, ah, void, and, ah, without 'form'. What do I mean by 'form'? First, God formed the mountains and the valleys and the dust of the ground, and then he tuck the dust of the ground and he formed Adam. Then he put Adam to sleep and he tuck a rib outen Adam and he formed Sister Eve, and the greatest formin' God ever did do was when he formed, ah, Sister Eve. And until this day when you sees a woman a walkin' down the street, and she's this-a-way in front, and that-a-way to the side, and down, ah, like this, if that ain't 'form,' what *is* 'form'!"

Sir Walter said one day a woman called him on the phone from a distant North Carolina town and wanted him to go down to Sanford and represent her daughter, who had been very badly treated. She explained that she could not come down, but wanted Sir Walter to get bond and try the case when it was called at the next term of court. He said the lady had a most pleasant voice and sounded as if she had just returned from a missionary meeting of the Ladies Aid Society of the Methodist Church, so he assured her that all matters would be attended to promptly.

He found out that the young lady was attending a
dance near a certain motel and that a gentleman passing through desired to join in the dance festivities. He
joined in, all right, but soon found that about $1200
was missing from his shoe or some other place of safe-
keeping when he became conscious next morning.

The young lady accused was the most innocent-look-
ing and demure young lady Sir Walter had ever seen.
She appeared to be greatly embarrassed by the matter
even being brought to court. She was forthwith released
from jail and when court was ready to convene about
two weeks later, Sir Walter met her at the bus station
and got a room for her at the hotel. He would bring her
back and forth to the courthouse in a taxi. She hardly
said anything and appeared very much in distress that
such a matter should ever be laid at her door. Sir Walter found out something about the man who had
brought the charges, and after he had made it known
what he was going to do in case the matter was prosecuted, the prosecuting witness sort of lost his taste for
the case and after a day or two in court the Solicitor
took a nol pros.

Sir Walter stood up in the court and thanked the
court, and his client bowed real low in a very gracious
and lady-like manner and shook hands with the judge.
Sir Walter escorted her out of the courthouse and got a
taxi and took her to the bus station and arranged for
her ticket and finally put her on the bus. He got her a
good seat and asked her to give his regards to her
mother.

The young lady walked back to the steps of the bus with him and as he started to leave, she reached up and kissed him on the side of his face and whispered into his ear these beautiful words: "Old man, you're a damn good mouthpiece."

Sir Walter said he was so put out he could hardly get back to the taxi, but he waved a sort of weak goodbye, doubting seriously that this client would attend any Ladies Air Society of the Methodist Church. But then we're living in strenuous times, and still she might.

Nobody knows what a woman is going to do, not even a woman. However, Sir Walter and I agreed that a woman will usually stick with a man better than a man will stick with a woman. Many women spoil men until they are almost unbearable. Then after they get unbearable, they do like Dr. Kinsey and write some kind of a report, which is just about all that it is, and most likely could be changed overnight. Sir Walter said though, that there was one paradox about women that he understood and that was that a man keeps running after a woman until she catches him. He also said that an affinity cocktail was just a drink with your sweetheart with your wife as the chaser. Sir Walter claimed that he believed that Solomon had a right extensive law practice as he had 700 wives and 300 stenographers.

CALL YOUR NEXT CASE.

18

SIR WALTER said that a man named
S. T. Paul one time stood in the midst of Mars Hill and
cried with a loud voice and said, "Ye men of Athens,
your gold is cankered and you're operating in the red,
and you're too superstitious, and you have gone and
put up a monument to the 'Unknown God'."

The truth about it is we are still operating under
the old superstitious ideas started by Satan at the first
meeting of the 4-H Clubs in the Garden of Eden. I
have actually seen born again, saved, Christians who
were in their own minds consecrated, who would dodge

around, rather than walk under, a ladder because it might mean bad luck. I remember telling Dr. William L. Pettingill, Pastor of First Baptist Church of New York City, "Goodbye, Dr. Pettingill, good luck."

He clouded up and frowned all over me and said, "Boy, don't say 'good luck' to me. That is a gambler's word. There is no such thing as good luck. God either permits a thing to happen, or he directs it to happen. When I leave you, say 'Goodbye, and may the Lord bless you'."

It made an "imprint" on me that I ain't never forgot. But superstition continues where people are outside Christ and the flesh is full of it, even among Christians. These things ought not to be, but when you walk up to newsstands, you will see a multitude of books trying to tell folks their fortune. They tell about which star you were born under, and all about the signs—whether they are in the head or in the feet. Sir Walter said he used to know some lawyers in the olden days down east (they are all dead now, of course) who had just one book in their law library—Blum's *Almanac*. He said if a man was coming up for trial and the signs were in the feet, it meant the case should be continued because if it wasn't, the client was sure to be sent to the roads. Some of these lawyers, he said, wore a left hind foot of a grave-yard rabbit on a large chain that hung across their middle, and it usually rested on that portion of the front where the vest failed to come down and the pants failed to come up, sort of a neutral position.

Sir Walter called these lawyers "Phi Beta Rabbit" lawyers. He said they would sit back in J. P. Court and fling that rabbit foot around, and bow and smile and look just as happy as if they were on salary. He said, in spite of all that you could do, every now and then one would make a motion before a justice of the peace for alimony *pendum litem,* and he had known of one fellow to take out claim-and-delivery papers for a house and had it jacked up and was going to move it onto another lot until he was stopped by a restraining order from a Superior Court judge.

He said one of these fellows told him one time that it made no difference to him if times did get hard and the law practice went to nothin'. "Let it get hard," he said. "What do I care? I'll fall right back on my notary public work."

Sir Walter said that as far as superstition was concerned, it was not altogether amongst ignorant folks, but was, in fact, even worse among the highly educated. All these Greeks that S. T. Paul was talking to were highly educated. The same condition exists among our highly educated folks today. Sir Walter said he walked into the bedroom of a Supreme Court Justice one day and flung his hat down on the bed, and the Justice said, "Hold on here. Don't do that! That is bad luck." And he grabbed up the hat and put it on the table.

I remember riding in a car one time with a man who had about all the degrees that he could get without turning into a thermometer. A black cat crossed the road going to the left, and he said, "Heavens! What will we do now? That is a sign of bad luck." So to take off the spell, he turned his hat around backwards. But he still didn't seem to have much confidence and worried all the whole trip.

Of course, if a screech owl hollers on the left side of the house between daylight and first dark, it is a bad sign, and about all that can be done at a time like that is to set an old shoe in the doorjamb and stick a pin in the wall. If he hollers the second night, you will have to sprinkle the shoe with punk water. Punk water is no good unless you get it right at midnight in a graveyard where they have quit burying folks. You usually find it in the top of an old hollow stump where it has rained and the water has caught in the top of the stump in that little rotten spot on top. Of course, if it is a very dry time, it is mighty hard to take the spell of a screech owl off to you and chances are the witches may ride you all over the country before you can get rid of the spell.

You can go to dinner with the most cosmopolitan and highly educated person in the country and after dinner if you try to light three on a match he goes into a frenzy. This same fellow can answer the $64,000 question without even studying the category, but he tips around all day long on the 13th, and moves uncommon slow, scared to death some goblin is going to get him because it is the 13th. Women are just about as bad as men. They'll buy all the books from the newsstand and read up on their horoscopes and fortune books, but you can't get them to read a short verse in the Bible. When people get bound down by superstition and refuse to trust the Lord, they inevitably do like old Saul did and consult the witches. It isn't any wonder that these fortune tellers can pay a license fee of $240 to engage in such business. Some even advertise over the radio. People in this country are truly fond of being defrauded. They love it and they will pay big prices for it.

Sir Walter said one time that it appeared to him that the people of this country had made up their minds to do three things, in particular: drink liquor, commit adultery, and gamble on something if it was only bingo at the Methodist bazaar. Knowing he was a Methodist, I never made no comment.

One time at a very exclusive country club social gathering, I killed a spider and started to throw his carcass into the fire, when a young lady, a graduate of one of our greatest universities, informed me that I should not do such a thing, as it was very bad luck. I did not do it because I imagine that the only thing that could take off that kind of a spell would be gopher dust.

Gopher dust is like first-class golf equipment—you can't get it except from a "pro." There are several Dust Doctors who operate in and around Chatham County, especially during a term of court, but the Seminary and seat of Higher Dust Doctoring is located between Bishopville, South Carolina, and Laurinburg, North Carolina. We had an old colored man at Carthage one time who got on the little train at Carthage and stood on the back platform and waved to all the folks at the station and said, "Goodbye, ol' North Carolina, I'm gone to Laurinburg"—which proves the location of the Seminary of Higher Dust Doctoring. At least it is in that direction.

Sir Walter and I were trying a manslaughter case at Carthage one time and during the noon hour a young woman, a high-school graduate, rushed into my office, and said, "Mr. Seawell, they have not only got Mr. Hoyle in my case, but they have employed a Dust Doctor, and every day at lunchtime he sprinkles gopher

dust on my runnin' board. Yesterday during lunch,
when a crowd was coming down out of the courthouse,
he got close to the judge and put some gopher dust on
the judge's coattail. And he says that this case of mine
where I am prosecuting Ed Dowd won't come up at
this term of the court at all."

Well, in the words of Dr. Needham Y. Gulley, I said,
"Let me see the color of your money."

She said: "It ain't to hunt."

So when court opened up after lunch, I got up and
made a motion to Judge Phillips and told him about
the Dust Doctor being in the courthouse, traveling
incognito and sprinklin' dust around. The Courthouse
all laughed and then Judge Phillips said, "Yes, I have
heard about that gopher dust business. I understand
that some was sprinkled on my coattail down at Laurinburg last week."

Then he turned to Mr. Roland Pruitt, the solicitor,
and said, "Mr. Solicitor, what is the number of this
case? Please mark it down for trial. I want it understood
right here and now we are going to try this case against
Dowd, gopher dust or no gopher dust."

Of course, it pleased my client and we all felt mighty
pleased and happy and satisfied and comfortable. But
what happened was, the court got tied up in a second-
degree murder case and the case against Dowd didn't
come up at all, and I have been reliably informed that
the Dust Doctor made more money at the next term
of court than the lawyers made. Sir Walter said it was
the dadburndest exhibition of gopher dust doctoring

he had ever seen, and if it would work against Judge
F. Don Phillips, it would might-nigh work any place.

*(Superstition is a terrible thing. Like sin, it is in the
bloodstream of all people of all generations—the ignorant, the highly-intelligent, the educated, the rich, the
poor, the good, the bad. All have sinned and come short
of the Glory of God. It is not trying, it is trusting. The
blood of Jesus Christ cleanses us from all sin. Thanks
be to God for His unspeakable gift.)*

CALL YOUR NEXT CASE.

19

SIR WALTER loved to take his pen in hand and write about the great patriots who lived in Chatham. Among some of the greatest that ever came out of Chatham, or remained in Chatham, was the London family. He wrote one special article about William Lord London, who was descended from John London, one-time secretary to Governor Tryon. His father and mother were Henry Adolphus London and Sallie Lord London. He was born in Pittsboro on April 3, 1838, and was the first North Carolinian to organize a bank in the State of North Carolina.

Sir Walter also liked to write about Colonel John Randolph Lane. He was the man who seized the flag of the Confederacy from the hand of Colonel Harry K. Burgwyn (uncle of Judge Burgwyn), who was mortally wounded during the battle of Gettysburg. He then carried the flag to the furtherest point in that battle. It was said by officers watching the battle to be the bravest act they ever saw.

Sir Walter said that the bravery of all the soldiers in the war was no surprise to him because it really took brave men to live in Chatham, and being brave came kind of natural-like. My grandfather and Colonel Lane were great friends, and so Judge Siler and I would talk over many of the old-time matters that happened back in those days. There was a considerable sprinklin' of what some folks called imagination, and others called just big lies. Maybe we did stretch it some, but we did enjoy it, and nobody knew enough to correct us much.

One day I was bragging to my wife (who is a considerable Yankee of strong character and fixed emotions) about the fact that I had five great-uncles in the battle of Gettysburg and three of them were killed. Instead of being impressed, as I was hoping she would be, she only asked the regular Yankee question: "How come they missed the other two?"

Speaking of bravery, it was Colonel Zeb Vance who remarked, while he was drawing up his troops for battle, that he was scared as a rabbit. It is said that while getting ready for the battle, a rabbit ran in front of Colonel Vance, and skipping down the field, disappeared in the brush and the Colonel said, "Go it, Molly cottontail, if I didn't have a reputation to sustain, I'd be with you."

Sir Walter said not many men are brave when they are all by themselves. But get up an army with some good leader and play music and sing songs and it helps to stir up a lot of courage that otherwise might fade away. One very strong general was getting ready for battle once, and a second lieutenant, seeing his hands shake, said, "General, I believe you are scared." The general replied, "I sure am, and if you were as scared as I am, you'd run."

Sir Walter told me one time that there was an old man, by the name of Peter Cockman, who lived over in Chatham County. He was talking to him about the War one time, and he said that the old gentleman confessed that he was with General Lee all through the War and called him "Bob," and he said he went to him one day and said, "Now, Bob, don't you never cross that there 'Tomac River. Over beyond that there river is Yankee tarritory. So don't never cross." But he said that Bob crossed over anyhow, and he went with him. "When we got over thar, we met them damn Yankees. Thar wuz any remount of 'em and they come from ever' correction. We tangled with 'em and they whupped hell outen us, and we wuz never wuth a damn atterward." Cockman added that he went to visit Bob after the War was over and when he got there, Bob asked him to come in and set a spell, and then they went down in the pasture for a walk and to take a look at old Traveler. They got to talking over old times and what-all was done in the War, and then they got down to Appomattox, and Bob asked, "Pete, was you there?"

"Bob, I shore was," answered Cockman.

"Well," said General Lee, "if I'd a-only knowed it, I would never have surrendered."

It is interesting to hear all these old stories that these oldtimers tell, and this state, we pray, will never lose its sense of humor, even in times of dire distress. You can never down a people who always see the humor in their most distressing times and seasons. If this country could ever elect a President who had a real genuine sense of humor, we could practically balance the budget his first year in office.

Sir Walter and I once had a case where we had made an effort to recoup for our client on a foreclosure matter. The mortgage holder had foreclosed on our client. He had gone upon his property and not only foreclosed on his real estate, but had seized his sawmill, which was not in the mortgage. He had actually gone in his yard and gotten his hogs and his chickens and all his farming tools which were not in the mortgage at all. The judge in the lower court had confirmed all these outrageous carryings-on, and we had appealed to the Supreme Court. The appeal was being heard over in the old Supreme Court room, which was across the street from where the present Justice Building is located. At the suggestion of Sir Walter, I said, among other things, that the only thing in history that compared favorably with the present foreclosure was Sherman's March to the Sea; and I thought that this method of foreclosure was worse, because it had purported judicial sanction up to the time of our appeal, and as far as I could find out, Sherman's March had never been approved by anybody, not even including Sherman.

About that time, Justice Clarkson raised his head and I knew I had hit on a tender spot. He began to tell about how the folks down here would have starved out if it hadn't been for cornbread and peas. So I let the reins down and gave him his head and let him travel. When he got through his discourse, Sir Walter says to me, with that steel-blue twinkle in his eye, "We done and won our case."

The reason the folks up North have forgotten about the War so quick and have no grudge about it is because they didn't have any property destroyed, houses burned, fields laid waste, or horses and cattle stolen. They were not cut down to cornbread and peas, not reduced to utter poverty. My grandmother told me one time that she had gone from Greenville to Wilson, North Carolina, in a beautiful carriage with four big black horses and a couple of footmen, and she and the others in the party were all dressed in the nicest of silk clothes and shoes. Five years later she made the same trip, riding in an oxcart, wearing a dress made out of old bagging cloth, a hat made out of cornshucks, and wearing wooden shoes. That kind of an experience makes a considerable impression on folks and they don't forget so easily.

When Henry Grady made his famous speech in Boston, some time after the War, he said he liked all the Yankees, he felt sure they were not near as mean as they had been pictured to him, and he believed that most of them were good folks. However, he would say that when Sherman went through Georgia, he was mighty damn careless with fire.

After the War was over, my two great-uncles, Uncle Jack and Uncle Ang Currie, came to live in Carthage and stayed with my grandfather most of the time. Uncle Ang sort of got over the War, but Uncle Jack looked with utmost suspicion on any stranger who appeared on the streets of Carthage. He felt certain that the Yankees would take over everything any day. My Uncle Jack was also a great talker and joketeller and was never quiet unless he was greatly disturbed about something. Usually, every Sunday, all the folks went to church at the old Presbyterian church which was only about two hundred yards from the house. After church there would be about fifteen or twenty to Sunday dinner, and they would all walk down through the old cedar walk about a hundred yards up to the house for Sunday dinner. Uncle Jack was usually the life of the party.

One Sunday he was very quiet and looked sick and disturbed. Finally one of my aunts asked him, when they sat down for dinner, "Uncle Jack, what is wrong with you? Are you sick? You have hardly said a word."

Taking his napkin and wiping his mouth, he asked, "Who in hell was that new man in the choir today?"

Sir Walter told me one time that some old man got to bragging about how tough the folks were when he was young, and he started to bragging about how he used to play football and finally he said he played in one great intersectional game that lasted four years and was later known as the Civil War. Which is somewhat like the story the man told about the time that George Washington put on his big show and threw the silver dollar over the Rappahannock River. He said a multitude of people came to the stadium, some had grandstand seats and others just stood and watched, and George came out with a big blue and red bathrobe on with a big white "W" on it, and warmed up awhile before making the throw. In the meantime, several vendors were selling cold drinks and beer and goobers, and they had a hard time getting the loudspeaker system to working, but finally they got Benjamin Franklin to charge the battery and things began to move along smoothly. But the thing that interested him mostly was a vendor selling a beer called "Molly Pitcher's Beer." He urged everyone present to get a pitcher of Molly Pitcher's Beer, because there was a pitcher of Molly Pitcher on the pitcher.

Sir Walter said one of the most interesting things to him was the fact that George Washington threw a silver dollar over the Rappahannock River, and along comes a man like Harry Truman, who threw five billion dollars over the Pacific Ocean. Throwing away money has been the theme of this country ever since.

Someone said, though, that if the liquor hadn't given

out, the South would have won the War. This is about as good as any other excuse since liberty and freedom, at the present time, are truly at a low ebb, and the question often arises as to whether or not this is really a free country. Which reminds me of the time that Sir Walter and some others were trying a civil matter in the courthouse at Carthage one very cold, cloudy, February day. Judge Hill, now deceased, was holding the court. The courthouse was about full of folks. Mr. Jackson, of the firm of Gavin, Jackson & Gavin, of Sanford, was standing up reading the pleadings to the Judge and jury. After he read a short while, a man stood up in the courthouse and said, "Read that last sentence agin."

"Are you a party to the case?" asked the Judge.

"No."

"Well, what do you mean, speaking out in the courthouse like that?"

"It's a free country, ain't it?" said the man. "Ain't a man got a right to hear what's goin' on?"

"You are in contempt of this court. Come up here."

The man staggered up to the bench and looked down at the Judge, and the Judge said, "What have you been drinking?"

There was a sort of a smile on his face as he replied, "Ever' thing."

"You are in awful contempt of this court," said the Judge.

About that time Talbot Johnson of the Moore County Bar, who is always trying to help folks, got to his feet and said, "If Your Honor please, I know this man. He is a fine fellow. He just came in here where it is warm. He didn't mean any harm. I used to hunt birds with him . . ."

About that time the man turned around from the bench and said, "Talbot, me and you has always been good friends and we are still good friends. But you keep out of this because me and the Judge are running our business."

"Sheriff McDonald," said the Judge, "Take him. Take him. He is in bad contempt."

Sheriff Charlie McDonald took him by the arm and led him outside the courtroom and started down the stairs, when the man asked, "Sheriff, what are you fixin' to do?"

"I am going to lock you up."

"Well, Sheriff, do you think that that judge has really got a right to do that to a man who is just trying to find out what's goin' on?"

The sheriff said he believed that he did have a right to do it.

"Well, Sheriff," said the man in an injured tone, "me and you has always been good friends, but if I'm locked up for trying to find out what is goin' on, this will be the damndest blow to liberty that I ever heard of."

CALL YOUR NEXT CASE.

20

SIR WALTER was the best hand in the world to mix up ancient history with current events. When he would tell about Washington crossing the Delaware, or Daniel Boone crossing into the Tennessee territory, it made you feel like it happened just about three days ago.

Sir Walter told how one time there was a man by the name of Julius Caesar who made quite a reputation for himself and got himself elected head of several countries at one time. Old Julius was a mighty easy-going kind of a man, but in his last days he had some serious trouble with his cabinet. Along about the last days of Julius, they held the Democratic National Convention in Rome and some of them put a wreath of some kind of flowers on Caesar's head, and it looked for certain that he would most likely run for a fourth term.

This made some of the cabinet mad, because most of them wanted to run, so they decided that in the name of liberty and freedom, Julius should be buried with great honors and the country saved.

Then, according to Sir Walter, one morning Julius parked his chariot in the parking lot in back of the Pentagon Building, wrapped his toga about him, and was on the way to his office down the hall when he met the Secretary of Labor, Secretary of Interior, Secretary of War, and Secretary of Agriculture, and other Secretaries too numerous to mention, and they crowded around Julius and let him have it. Before he was cut down by the Cabinet, in the name of liberty and international goodwill, Julius had written a book, sort of on the order of "One World," in which he declared that "All Gaul is divided into three parts." Sir Walter said that in the days to come, when the historians begin to write about the rise and the fall of the American Empire, it would be shown that the integration and the disintegration of America was divided into three parts. They will state that at one time "all America was divided into three parts, the DRIVES, the DRIVERS, and the DRIVEN." Doubtless, when the historian of the future shall essay to chronicle this great period of

American annals, some Livy, Tacitus, Macauley, Gibbon, H. G. Wells, or Jule Warren, who shall take his pen in hand to perform this task, will be moved to declare that at this period in the history of the United States, life was made up of three constant elements—the Drives, the Drivers, and the Driven.

Everything in this country has been put to the norm of dollars and cents. We measure everything in dollars. Any war leaves a multitude of ills in its wake, and among these come all kinds of agencies to relieve mankind, and while money can't buy happiness, it can move you a long way from misery. The result it reaches is that everybody, colored and white, yellow and tan, sooner or later gets tied up with a Drive.

Some Drives are good. We had to have Drives to sell War Bonds, keep up the Red Cross, Salvation Army and Polio Research and many others, but out of this has come all kinds of Drives. We have reached the time when Drives are about as numerous as political panaceas for saving the country. There is no community so deep in the hinterlands of the nation that it is not likely to become the birthplace of a Drive. There is no person so obscure that he may not successfully organize a Drive, and even though he is so little regarded that no one would ask him the time of day, he will soon be occupying the driver's seat and wearing a general's uniform and giving out orders like Stonewall Jackson.

Nowadays, even if a nameless billygoat, in his hasty meandering from his pastoral domicile to an adjacent turnip patch, should suffer the loss of a segment of his whiskers while crossing a barbed wire fence, immediately some kind of palpitating patriot starts a Drive to raise funds with which the owner may purchase a supply of Mexican Liniment and a cargo of Dr. J. Bird's Beard Restorer.

Sir Walter said, several years ago, that you couldn't have a Drive unless you had some Drivers, so the way to get a Drive started is to hire a brass band, call a meeting in the courthouse, raise a flag or two, open with a prayer, sing two or three verses of "Onward Christian Soldiers," call it the GRAND RALLY, appoint committees, especially appoint a Ladies Auxiliary, take up a collection, hold a bathing beauty contest, get Thad Eure to make the opening remarks (he'll come for nothin'), get Senator Kerr Scott to appeal to the farmers, and Senator Clyde Hoey to sound off the conclusion with a special appeal to God, the country and the Methodists in particular, and you've got a Drive started that all Hell can't stop.

When a Drive gets started, it is like a snowball rollin' down hill, getting bigger and gaining momentum all the time. From a small beginning, if properly nurtured and encouraged, it will soon cover the whole earth. Sir Walter said that sometimes a Drive breaks out in the most unexpected places. If someone suffering from cultural pains ascertains from reading Blum's *Almanac* that the musical genius who wrote the soulful tune, "Yes, We Have No Bananas," has a birthday, or someone discovers the date that the author of "Lay That

Pistol Down, Babe" was shot and killed by his sweet-heart, then someone gets up a great Drive with a GRAND BANANA DINNER AND PISTOL DAY LUNCHEON!

Let a strike break out among the wooden nutmeg manufacturers of Connecticut and a Drive is started at once to feed their starving families. Let a boll weevil from Mexico cross the border, and at once a Drive is started to finance an investigation to see if a commission should not be appointed to go to Mexico and study the problem on the local level.

The folks who really suffer from these Drives are those known as the Driven. When a Driver calls on you and explains all the strong points of the Drive, and how if you don't subscribe, you're not a good citizen, and how you will come down with the Seven Year Itch if you don't subscribe and give until it hurts, and how unchristian it is *not* to give, not many folks have courage enough to draw the line, and most are too weak in character not to run with the crowd.

The Drivers run over the Driven like a steamroller over blades of grass, and the only hope left for the Driven is that they can take at least part of it off the income tax. The most dangerous place to get hit by a Driver is in your office, but no place is safe. You can't quietly sit down in your own home and look at your television, and learn how to cure your colds and pneumonia with Vick's VapoRub, without some Driver interrupting. And if they can get some Governor or some Senator to say a word for the Drive, they may take a half hour or more and knock the whole program off the air. You can't listen to how the Durham Life Insurance Company craves to protect your family; or how anxious the Standard Oil Company of New Jersey is that you have happy motoring; or learn where the yellow went with Pepsodent; or what happened to Sally Patica; or if your snuff was too strong or if it was wrong, without being interrupted with some Governor or Senator reminding you that this is National Kiss Your Own Wife Week, and don't forget to contribute.

Sir Walter said that one of the special Drivers to watch is that man who appears at Sunday School and calls everybody "Brother" and speaks about Saint Paul as though he went to school with him. He said that most times you would find that this kind of a Driver was a real estate man who was anxious to sell an old swampy lot to the church for a parsonage or a recreational building.

The folks of this country have certainly been driven by all and sundry in years past—first by the British, then the Indians, the Mexicans, the Spaniards, the Yankees, the Carpetbaggers, the Scalawags, the Republicans and the Democrats, and others too numerous to mention. But we haven't given up hope. Some day a man with unusual powers of organization will organize a Drive to Drive out the Drivers.

Judge Way stood in the midst of his greenhouse near Southern Pines. A Driver approached him and asked him to contribute a dollar. The Judge, putting his

hand to his ear, asked him what he said. The Driver
went around on the other side, "I want you to contribute five dollars to the cause."

"Come back around on the dollar side," said the
Judge.

> Breathes there a man with a day so rare
> That no one tries his coin to share
> Nor seeks to relieve him of his hoard
> Together with his bed and board?
>
> Who ne'er hath met the Driver bold
> And heard his tale so grandly told
> When he, equipped with a line of bull
> The victim's leg essays to pull?
>
> If one so rare there chance to be
> In earth or sky or land or sea
> Go hunt him up and him salute
> For he is sure one blessed brute.
>
> And though he dies in rags, unknown
> Away from friends and all alone
> He'll be assured of endless rest
> Ne'er troubled by the Driving pest.

CALL YOUR NEXT CASE.

21

SIR WALTER told me one time that Chatham County sent more than two thousand soldiers into the Confederate Army, and considering the population of Chatham in the 1860's, that was quite a number. Back in 1924, the *Chatham News* published in a weekly series, "Biographical Sketches of Prominent Sons of Chatham." The series was written by Sir Walter. He wrote: "Chatham has produced many citizens whose distinguished public services and worthy lives have reflected honor upon the place of their birth. In this column there will appear each week a short biographical sketch of some son of the county, now dead, whose name should not be forgotten."

Many of the sons of Chatham who served in the war became high ranking officers, but only one general came out of this Chatham group. I have recently passed through Mobile, Alabama, and was interested to see there the name of a man from Chatham who was very successful in Alabama. He was General Isham W. Garrott, born in Chatham County, February 7, 1816 and educated at Pittsboro Academy. He became a lawyer, served the State of Alabama in both branches of the legislature of that state, and was killed in the Battle of Vicksburg.

Sir Walter Siler had started a history of Chatham County just prior to his death, and was not able to finish this work. But through the sketches he wrote, the history actually exists. Back when the sketches were written, Junius Wrenn was president, and J. B. Whitley, secretary-treasurer, of *The Chatham News.* The sketches are a very interesting piece of work and took considerable research, and I hope that Al Resch, present editor, or someone connected with this paper, will compile them into pamphlet or book form. If all the heirs of the folks named should buy the book, sales would reach into the thousands and the work would pay for itself many times over. Sir Walter often said that one of the best ways to go forward was to look backwards every now and then.

(We must all look backwards to the Cross to be saved, and then look forward to the Risen Christ, in order to walk as we should as Christians.)

Sir Walter loved to write about these good citizens of Chatham, because he was born and raised in Chatham and the history of the folks of Chatham was in his blood. The first house in Siler City that had glass for window panes was owned by a man named Siler. Part of the house was torn down and moved to Southern Pines in Moore County, and in later days was a part of the first liquor store established in Moore County. This was just after the Roosevelt Revolution, and subsequent to the days of the Noble Experiment.

One of the most interesting things about Chatham County is that it had a courthouse and was bearing down on folks for taxes a long time before it was actually a county. It is very interesting indeed to note that Chatham had a Clerk of the Court prior to the Revolution, who was issuing executions and writs of possession and other forms of oppression before Chatham was what we know now as Chatham. As mentioned earlier, this Clerk, William Hooper, signed his executions and writs in the name of King George the Third. Later he signed the Declaration of Independence, declaring that King George the Third was a tyrant, who didn't have sense enough to run this or any other country. This was a hanging offense, so far as George the Third was concerned, and it isn't any wonder that Ben Franklin told the boys in Philadelphia that all the signers would either have to hang together or they might hang separately. Chatham County is justly proud of the fact that it had a citizen and resident who put his name to the great document, even if it was a hanging offense.

Sir Walter told me one time that in speaking to the Daughters of the American Revolution, he reminded them that in order to get into their organization it was necessary for a member to prove that she was a direct descendant of a man, who, if he had been caught, would have been hanged for treason. He said some of the DAR's didn't have much sense of humor and got highly offended. Of course, it isn't so much what you do but how you do it, and it isn't so much what you say, but how you say it. For instance, if one man advocates the overthrow of the government by force of arms, be he a Communist or otherwise, we seize him and hang him. But if he can get enough folks to follow him, and a whole portion of the country rises up and secedes from the Union, and he gets up an army on the order of Lee and Jackson, then, even if he is defeated he goes down in history as a great hero. We erect monuments to such men, celebrate their birthdays, brag on 'em considerable, declare holidays, close banks and post offices, and all that kind of stuff. This, of course, is all right, but when you analyze the thing, it does seem foolish. But as Windy Billy Henderson said one time, the whole human race is a "dark and forbidding spectacle, too fraught with potentialities to be diagnosed with the analyticals."

I do not know how many of the good native sons of Chatham Sir Walter wrote about, but I will present at least a partial list. Most folks in Chatham are descended from these men:

Captain Laban R. Exline, Frank H. Woody, Richard

Carney Cotton, Mial Scurlock, William P. Taylor, Thomas West Harris, William Anderson Guthrie, John H. Haughton, Nathan A. Stedman, Richard Bray Paschal, Judge Thomas Brown Womack, Oran Alston Hanner, William Albright, William Smith McLean, Stephen W. Brewer, Justice Mathias E. Manley, John Manning, John Randolph Lane, Abraham Haywood Merritt, John S. Guthrie, William Brockley Stokes, Daniel Hackney, Hugh McQueen.

Vernon Patterson of Charlotte once told me that shortly after integration got on the minds of a lot of folks, two colored brothers met on the street corner in Montgomery, Alabama, and one said to the other, "Boy, I is done and traced up my family tree."

"What is dat you is done and chased up a tree?" asked the other.

"Boy, not chased up a tree, *traced* up a tree . . . yo' family tree, where all yo' folks come from."

"Don't try to tell me none of that stuff," said the second man. "They ain't but two kinds of things lives in trees. One is birds and the other is monkeys, and, boy, I don't see no feathers on you!"

(We are all proud of our ancestors; we have great hope for posterity, but we should always remember that no man should think too highly of himself, but think soberly, and as God hath dealt to every man the measure of faith.)

CALL YOUR NEXT CASE.

22

SIR WALTER knew Chatham like the palm of his hand. We would often talk about the great phenomenon of Chatham, the Devil's Tramping Ground (pronounced Trawmpin' Groun'). It lies in the southwest section of Chatham. It is a clearing about two hundred feet in diameter and has a rim to it about eighteen inches wide where nothing will grow, not even and including moody grass. It has been said that you can take moody grass and dig it up and burn the roots, but if you scatter the ashes it will grow again as soon as it rains. The rim of the Devil's Tramping Ground is bound to be under a curse, when not even moody grass will grow in that little rim that circles the circle.

Sir Walter said there was an old man who lived up in the west of Chatham many years ago, who could see the wind, and it was this old man who said that one night he saw the Devil out there walking around his trawmpin' groun' and talking to himself. Sir Walter said he believed the Devil used this trawmpin' groun' to rest up and meditate awhile after he was wore out with operations down in Lee and Harnett Counties.

That Harnett County should be pronounced "Hornet" County is insisted upon by those who really know the special language of the place. Some of the best folks that ever lived in North Carolina came from Harnett and many of them live there now. Doctors, lawyers, educators, big businessmen—like Nathan Johnson—are well represented. I walked into a drugstore in New York City one day and saw on the counter some candy made in Harnett County, at Dunn, by Wellons Candy Company. But good old Harnett has borne the brunt of many a joke. Sir Walter loved to use his wit on the boys of "Hornet" County. He said one time that "Hornet" County was one of the roughest counties in the state, that they had a town down there named "Anger."

He told me about the two old gentlemen of "Hornet" who were talking about sin. They argued back and forth for awhile, demonstrating their knowledge of the subject. Finally one old man said, "You think that sin started in the Garden of Eden, but it didn't. It started in Heaven when Lucifer the Angel of Light sought to be equal with God and lifted up himself in pride. And God made him the Devil and cast him down into the earth. You didn't know that, did you?"

"Didn't *know* it!" exclaimed the other. "Of course, I knew it. I not only knew he was cast down, I know where he hit the ground. It was over here in Hornet County about half way between Lillington and Dunn!"

Sir Walter used to love to tell that story, especially after he had read in the paper of some fresh outbreak down in Harnett involving the criminal laws. He used to say that it was no wonder that the devil always returned to his trawmpin' groun's in Chatham after a rough week end in Lee and Harnett. He needed to rest up and lay plans for the future. In Chatham County the Devil had a rather hard time operating because his first lieutenant, Mr. Liquor, was always kept on the run by John Emmerson, the high sheriff, and his good deputy, "Lace" Johnson. These two gentlemen operated on the theory that if you could head off the Devil's supplies, you could keep him under reasonable control. This works pretty well, but it is no guarantee at all, even in Chatham. So when some Chathamite insisted on getting drunk every week end, Sir Walter would usually order him to spend thirty days in the cooler, three days at a time, Friday, Saturday and Sunday. This is a pretty good system and ought to be invoked more often.

So far as sobriety is concerned, Chatham County has been a better than average county. I heard my father say one time that when he was solicitor he went down east to prosecute the docket and with him was a very good and pious judge of the Superior Court, and when he ordered the sheriff to open court, he did so in a completely abandoned and uninhibited manner. The judge called my father up to the bench and said, "Seawell, isn't our sheriff intoxicated?"

My father replied, "Yes, Judge. But the last time I was down here the sheriff and clerk were both pretty intoxicated. So we're making a 100 per cent improvemen."

Intoxicated or sober, some of our oldtime sheriffs and clerks were the souls of honor and most of them did a very good job. Sir Walter said that one day after the Devil had made a few rounds over in the trawmpin' groun', a cyclone hit the courthouse in Pittsboro and blew the roof off, and the only ones who didn't flee were the presiding judge and the defendant. The judge said that he was too scared to run, but since it presented such a magnificent opportunity to the defendant, and he didn't take advantage of it and refused to run, he would enter a verdict of "not guilty" and release the defendant. This, of course, proves the old adage that it is an ill wind that blows no good. Since the Devil, according to Scripture, is said to be the prince of the power of the air, this story takes on a high degree of most likely.

Getting drunk and serving the Devil has been one of man's chief occupations for a long, long time. Science has now come forward with a suggestion that getting drunk is just a disease. There is no cure for it, and no vaccination possible. Sir Walter used to love to tell the story about the woman who tried to cure her husband of drinking. She dressed up like the Devil and met her husband in the road when he was coming home in his usual condition. When she jumped out at him to try to scare him, he jumped back as though he was scared and asked who it was. She said in a disguised voice, "I'm the Devil." Quick as a wink came the response, "Shake hands, I'm pleased to meet you. I married your sister."

Sir Walter also liked the one about the man who was attending a very high-toned lecture by a famous world traveler. The lecturer was bragging considerable on where-all he had been and what-all he had seen, when a man about three-fourths in the wind asked him if he had ever had the delirium tremens. When the lecturer said he hadn't, the man told him, "You ain't been nowhere, and you ain't seen nothin'."

Sir Walter picked up a good story one time while he was up in Mount Airy. It seems that court was in session at Dobson and all the lawyers and the judge had their meals at a large table which seated about twenty folks. All the food was placed on the table and everyone sat down and began to help themselves. For Sunday dinner at this boardinghouse, there had been a large turkey, and the old bird was pretty well picked over by the time court met on Monday. In spite of this, at every meal they would bring in the turkey carcass and set it right in the middle of the table. This was done at every meal all through the week. Finally on Friday at noon, when the old bird's bones were again laid on the big platter and set in the middle of the table, an old mountain lawyer, who was gradually getting drunker as the term of court proceeded, sat down at the table, and seeing the old bird laid out again, got a big carving knife and stuck it down through the carcass, and in a deep bass voice said, "Do you acknowledge yourself indebted to the State of North Carolina in the sum of fifty dollars, out of your goods and chattels surely to be assessed if you shall fail to make your appearance here at the next term of this court?"

Sir Walter was a bosom friend of J. C. B. Ehringhaus, one of North Carolina's best-loved Governors and a most delightful gentleman of the old school. He said that when the Governor was practicing law down in Elizabeth City, he had a very good lawyer friend, named Darb, who was an old bachelor and inclined at times to get right much in his cups. However, he would never be seen in public when under the influence, and would go straight to his hotel room and get in bed. He said that on one occasion Darb went to the hotel, but was rather late arriving, and in his confusion got into the room of a middle-aged lady who was also living at the hotel. When she opened the door and saw him in her bed, she let out a scream and called the hotel manager. He came up and saw at once what the situation was, and in a tactful way asked the good gentleman to get up and get out. But the tippler had gotten the idea that they wanted to get him out on the street so that some of his friends could seize him and send him to Keeley. He therefore refused to budge. When the manager told him he was in the wrong room, he wouldn't believe it. "I am in my room and I am going to stay here," he said. Several friends went up and tried to get him to move, but to no avail. In desperation they sent for the Governor.

Sitting down by Darb's bed, Governor Ehringhaus said, "Now listen to me. You are in the wrong room."

"You are just trying to fool me, this is my room," came the reply.

"I'll show you something," said the Governor. Pointing to the dresser, he said, "Look at all those feminine things on that dresser."

"That's just a trick you're trying to pull on me."

The Governor rose from his chair and opened the

closet door. "Now look at all these feminine things in this closet. This is *not* your room."

"That's just another trick. I came to my room and put on my nightgown and got in this bed and you are not going to fool me out of it!"

The Governor returned to his seat by the bed, and pulling down the counterpane, took hold of a thin lace-covered pink nightgown. He pulled it up to Darb's face and said, "Now look, what have you got to say about this?"

After looking at the pink nightgown for awhile, Darb finally spoke, "Now, that," he said, "is the first piece of *competent* evidence you have offered."

That Sir Walter and Governor Ehringhaus were keen friends manifested itself quite often, for they exchanged witticisms every time they met. The sales tax was passed during the administration of Governor Ehringhaus and those who cussed it out most wouldn't repeal it. The Governor was a good lawyer and a positive sort of a man, and he often referred to his political enemies as mugwumps, and said that a mugwump was a political bird who sat on a fence with his mug on one side and his wump on the other.

The Devil, I guess, still operates his trawmpin' groun' over in Chatham, but Sir Walter and the man who could see the wind have gone on. One of the greatest preachers of the Gospel who ever lived was Dwight L. Moody. Standing and looking at a drunk lying in the ditch one day, he said, "But for the Grace of God, there lies Dwight L. Moody."

God defeated the Devil at the Cross. He will save all those who come to him by the way of the cross. The blood of Jesus Christ, God's Son, cleanses us from all sin. The amazing thing is that folks won't believe it. But then the Lord himself said one time, they won't believe it though one rose from the dead.

The Devil is still in his Trawmpin' Groun', not only in Chatham, but all over the world. But one day the Lord will return and then the lion and the lamb will lie down together, and nothing shall hurt them in all my holy mountain for the knowledge of the Lord shall cover the earth as the waters cover the sea.

CALL YOUR NEXT CASE.

23

SIR WALTER told me that he once took a trip out West. He took a train in Chicago and traveled to Washington, Montana, California, Old Faithful, the Grand Canyon, Yellowstone and other places too numerous to mention. But he said he wouldn't swap good old Chatham County and Hickory Mountain fresh air for all things west of the Mississippi. So far as he was concerned, the West was oversold. It reminded him of the colored woman who came to his office one day and said, "Mr. Jedge Walter, I desires for you to get me a disvorce."

"Why, Mary," he said, "I understand that you just got married about three weeks ago. What is wrong?"

"Well, Mr. Jedge," replied Mary, "if you must know, I will say that that was the most over-introduced colored brother I ever met."

It is good to advertise places and it is good to read about the West and many of the wonderful sights, but the truth is that back in Chatham County things are green and pretty and lovely compared to the rocks and dust and smog that I have seen out there. In Chatham the air is fresh and invigorating, and I can understand now why Sir Walter said he wouldn't swap Hickory Mountain for all the western air with so much body to it. People in Chatham, according to the Judge, didn't really know how to appreciate what they had until they saw some other places where mankind has overrun nature and made mostly a manufacturing mess of his local environment.

Not appreciating what you have at home until someone points it out to you, is sort of like the joke Sir Walter told about the colored woman in Chatham who married a mighty good colored man and they had lived together for about fifteen years. He was a good provider and they seemed to have a very happy home and to all outside appearances they were getting along very nicely together. One day, however, a strange wayfaring colored brother dropped into town and the first thing anybody knew, the colored lady had joined him and they were soon seeking legal advice and asking how to get a divorce. The Judge asked her why she would leave her good husband and take up with this kind of a man. "Your husband is a steady provider and makes good money and has always been kind to you. Why do you want to take up with this old sort of a tramp of a man and run off with him?"

"Mr. Judge," she said, "I know you is tellin' me the truth, but this here man you calls a sort of a tramp has done and found love and appreciation about me that I didn't even know I had."

The good folks in Sir Walter's domain of Chatham County, if they will just look about them, will find that they have 'most everything that any folks could want, and a lot of stuff they didn't even know they had. It is no wonder that Sir Walter often said he wouldn't swap Rocky River for the Rio Grande nor Siler City for Las Vegas. It is true, of course, that the grass always looks greener on the other side of the fence, but Sir Walter had crossed the fence and found that the real green grass of a community is usually growing right under your own feet.

After I had been in the Far West for three days, and having seen only rocks and dust and sagebrush, an old blackjack in Chatham became a really beautiful tree. Of course, out there they do have some green places, and when they put water to their old dusty ground, it will really produce. They do have some scandalously large trees also, but for every acre of green and trees there are one thousand acres of rock and dust, and on most of the land you can't even raise an umbrella. When I saw all this old poor land out there, and all the rock and dust, I began to dream about good old Kinston, North Carolina, and all the black farm land around old Bucklesberry, and how down there when they plant cucumbers they throw out the seed and run into the house right quick to keep from getting tangled up in the vine. It is all right to be a sort of cosmopolite and have a metropolitan outlook, up to a certain extent, so folks won't think we are too provincial. But, after all, the real aristocracy of this country are those folks who are able to stay at home and live on the land. Most folks think that it gives them polish to move around all over the country and visit everything, including Europe in particular. Which reminds me of what Sir Walter said about a colored brother who was sitting on a bench up in Harlem looking awful sad and melancholy, when another brother approached him and said, "Boy, what is wrong with you? You look awful sad. You ain't sick, is you?"

"I ain't sick," replied the other, "but I is worried because I is so far from home."

"Where is yo' home, Boy?"

"If I told you, you wouldn't know. I is a *long* ways from home."

"Well, tell me whar it is."

"I is all de way from Raleigh, Nawth Cawlina."

"Boy, is you really from Raleigh? I'se from Raleigh, too! What street did you live on?"

"Gaston Street."

"Why I did too! What number was it?"

"Number 640 Gaston Street."

"Six-forty! Man! Upstairs or downstairs?"

"I lived upstairs."

"I did too. Did you work daytime or nighttimes?"

"I worked daytimes."

"Well, I worked nighttimes. Did you know Mae Belle Jones?"

"Sho!"

"Well, boy, shake hands with me. You and me is husbands-in-law!"

Colonel Risden Tyler Bennett, an oldtime lawyer from Wadesboro, said one time that he wouldn't believe anything that an expert witness would say because one swore him out of court one time. He said that an expert witness was one that would tell more and more about less and less and swear to it in a haphazard sort of manner and in such a careless way that even the judge would get to believing what the fool was saying. Speaking to a jury one time in Wadesboro, Colonel Bennett made some remarks like this: "Gentlemen of the jury, we are confronted in this case with the statements of a man who calls himself an expert witness. The court has ruled that he is an expert, and I reckon he is. But as for me, I would never believe anything that one of these expert witnesses says. They will actually go on the witness stand and swear to you how far it is from here to the moon. As far as I know, no one has ever been to the moon and no one from the moon has ever been down here. But these experts will tell you how far it is and give it to you in feet and inches, if necessary. Now you can believe that stuff if you want to, but before I would believe how far it is from here to the moon, I would have to see the heavens open, and two white-clad angels come from the moon to the earth with a surveyor's chain in their hands, the front angel a-hollerin' 'Stake!' and the 'hind angel a-hollerin' 'Stuck!', before I would believe how far it is from here to the moon."

Sir Walter was always wanting the folks of Chatham to be more enlightened about their county and state. For this reason, he would do a lot of speaking and also a lot of writing about Chatham and North Carolina. Nothing made him happier than when he was commenting on current events or some event in history which was connected with Chatham County and the great State of North Carolina. However, in spite of all you can do, most folks are not much interested in history, and much less in current events, unless they get run over or slapped down in the process. He often remarked that most folks just don't care where they came from or where they are going. It is hard to get their attention, and even after you get their attention, they don't know what you are talking about.

Which reminds me of the time the man lent his mule to a friend and told him that he would not have to whip him or strike him, but only speak to him. After awhile he went out to see how he was getting along

and saw the man knock the mule down with a large
stick.

"What do you mean hitting my mule? I told you all
you had to do was speak to him," he said.

The other man replied that he understood that all
right. "I was just trying to get his attention," he said.

Sir Walter said that you could make an effort to get
folks to love their county and state more, but sometimes you just have to wait until they sort of get caught
up with themselves so that they can really appreciate
the fact that those living in Chatham and the great State
of North Carolina have been greatly blessed of the
Lord. He said that sometimes the attitude of folks
about their own home and surroundings reminded him
of the old colored man who was brought before him for
trial. He asked him if he had a lawyer. He didn't. He

asked him if he wanted him to appoint him one, and the old man replied, "Jedge, I was up one time over in Federal Court and that jedge over dere appointed a lawyer to recommend me, and you know what that jedge done? That jedge put me in jail and turnt dat lawyer loose. I don't believe I want nary lawyer to recommend me no more. I is jest decided to throw myself on the ignorance of this here court."

When we travel afar and think we have a chance to discover some pasture greener than North Carolina and Chatham County, we have just thrown ourselves upon the ignorance of ourselves.

CALL YOUR NEXT CASE.

24

SIR WALTER said that he used to get up early in the mornings and stick his head out the window and get that fresh aroma of wonderful Chatham air coming down off Hickory Mountain, and he said it made him feel mighty good to be in Chatham. He said he would then look toward Tick Creek and then look back toward old Rocky River and then look over toward Mount Vernon Springs, and begin to get that great realization that he truly was dwelling in God's Country.

By this time, he was ready for breakfast, and after some good country ham and eggs, and two cups of hot coffee, he would go down to the post office and get the mail and then go to his office and read the editorial page of the *News and Observer,* and then immediately come down with cirrhosis of the liver. He said that everybody in North Carolina loved the *News and Observer,* and everybody, down east especially, read it; but there were times when such reading brought on convulsions of all types.

The Daniels family of North Carolina has been a great asset to the state. It is perhaps the best known family in North Carolina, and no family was ever loved and cussed out as much. Usually, folks in public life are loved by some and cussed out by others, but no family in North Carolina became more distinguished on a national scale than the Josephus Daniels family of North Carolina.

Sir Walter told me one time that he always read everything that Mr. Joe Nathan Daniels wrote. He called Jonathan "Joe Nathan" because that was the way that the colored folks pronounced it, and of course, we must be in tune with our times. He said he enjoyed everything Mr. Joe Nathan wrote because he realized that it took years of hard work, research, and a magnificent education for any man to be able to write the kind of narrow-minded, prejudiced stuff that he wrote.

Sir Walter used to call me on the phone and say, "Seawell, it's about time for us to go over to Raleigh and get some of our legal matters over there straightened out."

I would say, "Judge, where are you?"

And he would say, "I am over here in Pittsboro, but I can meet you down in Sanford."

"Oh, no!" I would say, "You stay right where you are and I will pick you up there. I can cut through the woods and come by Bear Creek and be there in solemn time.' '

From thence, we would proceed to Raleigh, and on the way, Sir Walter would tell me all about how close the capital of North Carolina had come to being in Chatham County, located on the peninsula between Deep River and Haw River, and how a lot of folks lost their shirts and underwear speculating on the land located around what was known as Haywood, and how later on they all got drunk at Merry Oaks, and that was how Merry Oaks got its name—which I guess is a reasonable kind of deduction and mostly true.

When we rolled into Raleigh, the Judge would say, "Seawell, let's go by and see the governor first. We might just as well start at the top and work down." It is a sort of a Republican attitude, but then it is easier.

We would usually go by and have a little chat with the governor and he would give us his latest joke. Governor Broughton said that a little girl had written him and wanted a pitcher, and he wrote and asked what kind and if she wanted one with a handle to it, or a glass pitcher, or a silver pitcher. And she had written back and said, "I don't want no glass pitcher or a silver pitcher, and I don't care nothin' about no handle. I just want a pitcher of you."

After visiting with the governor, Judge Siler would say, "Now, let's visit our Secretary of State, Thad

Eure," although he didn't call him Thad Eure. He called him Thadimonius Euripedes, which seemed to fit him pretty good, because he had been in office ever since Caesar had crossed the Blue Ridge. After telling his favorite joke, Thadimonius Euripedes would usually show us his new spring hat, which was direct proof that spring was only about two weeks off. Thadimonius Euripedes wanted always to be first in hats, but his real first love was votes, and he knew how to get them, and a more likable Roman never lived.

From the office of the secretary of state, Sir Walter would next call on his old friend, Chief Justice Stacy. They used to room together in Raleigh back in the old days when Sir Walter served as assistant attorney general of North Carolina. It was a liberal education to sit and hear these two gentlemen talk current events and history and the news in general, and old times in particular.

Sir Walter pointed out to me, over in the old Supreme Court Building (not the new Justice Building), that the only plaque set up in that building was one erected to a man who served a term in the penitentiary—O. Henry. Sir Walter said that he doubted if O. Henry would ever have written anything at all if he hadn't been shut up in jail so he couldn't do anything else. John Bunyan, he recalled, was arrested for speeding and served quite a while, otherwise we might not have had the wonderful book, *Pilgrim's Progress*. This proves the old adage that it is an ill wind that blows no good, or words to that effect.

Which recalls the time that Judge Adams of Carthage was cross-examining an old colored man named Handy Kidd. After Judge Adams had raked Handy over the coals a time or two, he pointed his finger at him and said, "Handy, I'll ask you, haven't you been in jail?"

Handy replied, "Yes, I've been in jail, but some mighty good folks have been in jail."

Judge Adams, not seeing the trap set for him, said, "Who's *good* that has ever been in jail?"

Whereupon Handy replied, "Paul and Silas was in jail."

After that, Judge Adams didn't dare ask him any questions.

After a conference with the Attorney General and other friends, we would usually go down the street and visit with some of the lawyers. Then, I would want to go by their office, and see my old friends, Clyde Douglass and Roy McMillan. We knew we could pick up some tall tales in this section of the jurisprudence in particular.

One of Clyde Douglass's favorites concerned the colored man who told how he was sitting on the steps of a house talking to another brother's best girl, when the other man came up from behind. "He hit me over the head with a two by twice and killed me."

"If he killed you," asked Mr. Douglass, "what are you doing here now?"

Whereupon he replied, "But, Mr. Lawyer, he didn't kill me *dade*."

Roy McMillan then told of the time two colored bishops were on the way to the Conference. They had a serious wreck with their car, and later one of the bishops was on the witness stand and he was asked to tell what happened.

"May it please Your Honors," he said, "we was traveling to the Conference in our automobile, when suddenly from a filling station on the left hand side of the road, this big Packard car, it swuved over onto our side of the road in a catawampus, antigodlin manner and hit us direct in front, and there was a great lamination and breaking of glass."

Mr. McMillan then asked him, "What happened after that?"

"May it please Your Honors," he replied, "I does not know. It was then that the book of my memory closed."

Sir Walter usually would not leave Raleigh until he had gone down and visited with his old friend Buck Jones, one of the best lawyers North Carolina ever produced. Folks used to say that if Mr. Buck Jones didn't win a case, he would tear the courthouse down. Usually when he spoke to the jury, you would think that it was really going to fall in. When we walked in, Sir Walter said, "Well, Buck, how are you getting on?"

"I'm sick," he said, although he was certainly the picture of health. "I have just been reading this *News and Observer,* and it looks like all the good folks around Raleigh are about to die out. It is distressing to see so many good folks leaving us, but the editor of this paper, confound him, he don't even get the toothache."

CALL YOUR NEXT CASE.

25

SIR WALTER was a great believer in the freedom of the press. He said that the freedom of the press helps to guarantee all our other freedoms. It is like the key log in a log jam. If it is ever destroyed, all the rest of our freedoms will go down the river to destruction. The gentlemen of the press loved Sir Walter and he loved them. They were a complement to each other. Whenever a newspaper reporter saw Sir Walter in circulation around Raleigh, or any other leading city in North Carolina, he always cheered up considerable, because he knew Sir Walter was good copy.

Many newspaper reporters would go and sit in the

courthouse and listen to Sir Walter try a case just to see him in action. Sir Walter had a way of puncturing a judge and letting the wind out of him, when it appeared that he was beginning to be a little puffed up, much to the delight of everyone in the courtroom, including the judge.

Sir Walter and I were walking down Fayetteville Street in Raleigh, when he said, "Seawell, look at Tom Bost coming yonder with his hat on the back of his head and his hair flying in all directions. He's eating peanuts out of a bag in his left coatpocket and he has a notebook under his right arm. He's looking all around like he doesn't have a bit of sense, when he's got more sense than anybody in Raleigh—unless, of course, it's us."

About that time we got close enough to speak, and Mr. Bost said, "Hello, Walter, what's up?"

Sir Walter said, "Tom, you follow us and you'll see what's up. We are on our way now to the great courthouse of Wake County where this battle will soon begin, and if you will listen, I will clue you in on the lawsuit of the century. We have brought a lawsuit for a group of patriots against those who would seek to violate Proverbs, and who would remove the old landmarks, and also in violation of Habakuk 2-12."

"Well," says Mr. Bost, "I know the old proverb 'remove not the old landmark,' but what in the world is Habakuk 2-12?"

So Sir Walter gave it to him, " 'Woe unto him that buildeth a town with blood, and establisheth a city by iniquity.' Our lawsuit is entitled Edgar R. Brown, J. Madison Hunsucker, Coy S. Lewis, and other patriots

too numerous to mention, versus a multitude of plutocrats who are seeking to change the old Anglo-Saxon
name of the town of Hemp, to one of Bavarian flavor
and call it 'Robinsky'. We shall fight this case through
all the courts of our land, and if unsuccessful, we shall
appeal to the Court of the Hague."

After hearing these remarks, Mr. Tom Bost got on
our trail and stayed with us throughout the entire liti-
gation. When we reached the courthouse, we were
joined by another great North Carolina journalist and
former editor, the great Oscar J. Coffin, commonly
known as "O. J.," "Ock" and "Cap Coffin." Sir Walter
gave him something to write about when he opened up
and expressed his contempt for those who would dare
to remove the old landmark or change the name of that
which had been long and well-established. Sir Walter
kept the courtroom in an uproar for about an hour.
Comparing the name of Hemp to that of Robinsky (he
wouldn't call it Robbins) was, he said, like comparing
the puny pelvis of a Peruvian prince to the brassbound
biceps of a Roman gladiator. He also said that he had
a lot in common with the name "Hemp." The name
Siler meant "ropemaker" and hemp and rope had a lot
of interest in each other.

The names of towns brought to mind the products
of those towns: when we say High Point, we think at
once of furniture; Boston reminds us of beans; Pitts-
burgh means steel; when we say "Reno" we think of
divorce; Washington, D. C., makes us think of confusion; and when we say Shelby, we think of Democratic candidates. (At that time about ten candidates

were running out of Shelby, and others were threatening to run.)

In conclusion, Sir Walter said all the plaintiffs, who were the patriots in the lawsuit, had ancestors who died like flies at Valley Forge, were riddled by cannon fire and bayonets at Gettysburg, and charged up San Juan Hill with Teddy Roosevelt. They had hovered over soup bowls with Hoover and suffered the loss of shoats with Henry Wallace, but before they would let any man change the name of Hemp to Robinsky, they would be like Jim Bloodsoe on the Mississippi, and hold the nozzle of the good ship Liberty and Freedom agin' the bank of deceit and adversity until the smokestack fell in.

At the conclusion of the above, Sir Walter informed the court that the word Hemp had nothing to do with rope, and was actually the contraction of "home place." Whether or not this was true nobody knew, but it sounded good and the judge looked like he believed it. Sir Walter then launched a discourse about the old home place and told about walking in the valley of despair with the chilling winds of adversity sweeping over his soul; like the prodigal of old when he thought of the old home place, he took new courage and was greatly refreshed; he knew that at the old home place a light was still burning in the window. And then he ended up on something about Mother Machree and gray hairs and fingers all careworn and gnarled, and all that kind of stuff. He actually did draw down a couple of tears out of the judge, but it didn't amount to anything. Some judges are like that. Sometimes I think they operate under the old maxim, "Rejoice with them that do rejoice and weep with them that weep."

Writing the next day in "Among Us Tar Heels," Mr. Bost said that not since the days of Fabius Busby had any man jarred the foundations of the Wake County Courthouse like Sir Walter had jarred 'em. And Mr. Coffin, writing in his "Shucks and Nubbins" said that Sir Walter was a sort of a cross between Macawber, Clarence Darrow and William Jennings Bryan, which is a reasonable deduction and seems to state the case.

For many months after this hearing, and the speech made by Sir Walter, you would often see something about him in the two writers' columns. One of the finest things about Mr. Tom Bost and Mr. Ock Coffin was the fact that if they liked you, they said so; and if they didn't like you, they also said so. Both of them were constantly striking at the pretense and sham that is always lifting its head in public life, especially by politicians and do-gooders.

Mr. Tom Bost one time made a trip down to my home. Mrs. Seawell was constantly raking him over the coals about some of the religious articles he wrote for the papers, but we rejoiced when he told us that he was a true believer, and that—regardless of what or how we interpreted his articles on religion—he believed that Christ died for our sins, according to the Scriptures, and that He was buried and that He rose again, according to the Scriptures. O. J. Coffin and Tom Bost will long be remembered by North Carolinians. These gentlemen of the press will not be replaced in our day and time, nor in a hundred years.

But getting back to the famous speech—as soon as Sir Walter finished his oration on changing the name of Hemp to Robinsky, and the courtroom calmed down and the judge dried his tears, and the shouting and the tumult faded away, the judge decided the case against us. We immediately gave notice of appeal, shook hands with the judge and departed to a cafe to get some refreshment. Sir Walter, after cooling off and eating a little bread and butter, said, "This case is headed straight for the Court of the Hague. There is an international principle involved here and these local courts are too provincial to handle such matters properly."

I asked him what he thought of the decision and he said that it reminded him of a case he had one time before a justice of the peace. When he finished that case, he asked for a decision, but the justice of the peace said, "No. I will not hand down any decision in this case today. I am going to take the case under advisement for about ten days. However, I will say this, that when I do hand down my decision, it will be against you."

After lunch, Sir Walter said, "Seawell, we will prepare our papers of appeal and continue to strike a few blows for liberty, but these Democratic plutocrats are mighty hard to beat." Looking at me with a twinkle in his eye, he said, "Almost thou persuadest me to be a Republican."

CALL YOUR NEXT CASE.

26

SIR WALTER used to circulate in Chatham with no uncertain circulation. Many things he said and did, concerning the noble folks of Chatham, went unheard, unhonored and unsung. He often said that an honest confession was good for the soul but rough on the reputation.

Sir Walter once entered a cafe in El Paso, Texas, and made a very serious faux pas. He entered the place in a very friendly manner and sat down at a table with some others present. In passing a few pleasantries, he asked one gentleman at the table where he was from and where he was going. To his utter surprise, everybody in the cafe made a quick exit. The proprietor explained to him that it was exceedingly bad manners in El Paso to ask any person where he was from or where he was going, and it was extremely bad manners to ask any person his name.

This brings to mind the story that Sir Walter told me about a man named Baily, a sheriff in western North Carolina. He told how, back in the days when Republicans had some hope of posterity, Baily had been elected sheriff of two counties. I think he said one was Madison and the other Buncombe. But after the Democrats rose in wrath and slew Hoover and ten thousand of his saints, Sheriff Baily went out West. The Sheriff later told Sir Walter that he stayed away about ten years, and one day he was back East and passing through Madison County, when he saw an old man on the side of the road thumbing a ride. He slowed down his car, stopped, and picked him up. When the old man got in the car, the first thing he said was, "Ain't you ex-Sheriff Baily?"

The Sheriff said, "No. I am a man named Smith. From out west."

The old man said, "You shore do look like him!" They rode on a little ways and the old man said, "Ain't you tryin' to fool me? Ain't you ex-Sheriff Baily? You are shore the spittin' image of him, and you even talk like him."

"My name is Smith," repeated Baily. "What kind of a sheriff was this man?"

"He was a good sheriff, all right," said the old man. "And he captured more liquor than any sheriff we ever had!"

Then Sheriff Baily asked, "Did he drink liquor, this sheriff you're talkin' about?"

"Oh no," replied the old man, "he didn't drink none at all. He just sold it."

Sheriff Baily told Sir Walter that after that statement he was truly Mr. Smith from way out west, and he durst not inquire further into the matter. Furthermore, down to this good day, he doesn't know whether the old man was foolin' him or he was foolin' the old man. It could have been a combination of both. Truly, the old man had the last word on the subject. When you try to fool some of our good old mountaineers in western North Carolina, it is best to be sure of your trap. Sometimes they will set a backfire that will smoke you out.

Sir Walter and I appeared in court in Asheboro one day while Judge Felix Alley was holding the court. He is the man who wrote "Musings of a Mountaineer." He had a magnificent sense of humor, and as we approached the bench, he rose up, and sticking his hand out to me, said in a loud voice, so all in Republican Randolph County could hear, "WHY, YOU OLD DEMOCAT, YOU!" After a few minutes, Judge Alley recessed the court, and all the lawyers and the Judge and Sir Walter retired to the Judge's chambers. Two

kindred souls had met. And when Judge Alley and Sir
Walter had finished their discussions of trials and trib-
ulations, politics and pollutions, peartenin' water was
not necessary and joy reigned supreme in the Randolph
courthouse. They were two men who had a great deal
in common, in their love for the Democratic Party, the
South, and the people of North Carolina in particular,
and nearly everything else in general. Both of them
enjoyed every minute spent in observing the conduct of
people. Judge Alley told how one time the government
put in a little post office way up on the Blue Ridge,
where one had never been before. After it opened, an
old mountaineer journeyed down out of the mountain
and went into the little wooden building, and asked if
he had any mail. The postmaster asked him what his
name was. "What you want to know that for?" asked
the old man. "Don't you know durn well if I git any
mail my name will be on the letter?"

Judge Alley also told us about the old mountaineer
who had the habit of taking on a little too much peartenin' water. One night right after dark, he stepped up
on the back porch of his little cabin. He was mighty
thirsty. His wife had already gone to bed, it being
rather late — about eight o'clock — and the house was
dark. But the old man found the waterbucket on the
little shelf on the back porch, and taking the gourd
dipper, he got a big drink and was gulping it down with
a considerable big swallow. His wife had dropped a
little ball of twine in the waterbucket and he swallowed
the whole thing, except a little piece of the string,

which hung out on the side of his mouth. Taking hold of it, he began to pull and the little ball began to unwind down in his stomach. He started staggering around on the porch, mumbling to himself.

"What is the matter with you out there, you old drunk fool?" called his wife.

"Polly," said the man, "don't speak mean to me now."

"What *is* wrong with you?" she inquired.

Still pulling on the string, and feeling it unwinding, he said, "Polly, I don't think I am going to be with you long."

"Can't you tell me what in the dinah is wrong with you?"

"If I ain't the worse mistaken I ever been in my life," he moaned, "I am a-unravelin' from the inside."

Judge Alley also told about the mountaineer who argued his case before the Supreme Court. This story provides a good illustration of the ability of the folks of western North Carolina to catch on their feet under any circumstances. In fact, all North Carolinians have a great sense of humor, and even when they are knocked off the limb, they all know how to land on their feet.

In Judge Alley's story, an old mountaineer was arguing a case before the Supreme Court. To prove some point, he began to talk about some phenomenon, only he didn't call it that. He called it a "phenonim." He was talking about the petrified forest, and he called it "peterfied."

His remarks went something like this: "If it pleases Your Honors, this here was the greatest phenonim that ever happened in this here country. Why, out thar in the West a whole territory become peterfied, the trees become peterfied, the bushes become peterfied, the grass become peterfied, and one day, if it pleases this Court, a pheezant was a-flyin' across thar, and lo and behold, he also become peterfied and there he hung between heaven and earth, peterfied."

The Court could stand it no longer, so one member asked, "Do you mean to stand there and tell this court that one day a pheezant, flying across that phenonim got halfway across there and become peterfied, and there he hung between heaven and earth, peterfied?"

The old mountaineer said, "That is right, Your Honors."

"Well, then," said the judge, "answer the Court one question. What happened to the law of gravitation?"

"Why," said the old mountaineer, "it was also peterfied at that time."

Judge Alley had another kindred spirit in Justice Carlisle Higgins. Both of them were mountaineers with that sharp sense of humor that you can't find except on rare occasion, but when you do find it, it is like a good cool drink of water on a hot, dusty day.

One of their favorites was the story about Cousin John and Cousin Bill, who lived up in the mountains. They used to ride down to a little barroom in the valley every night and play cards and get reasonably drunk until about closing time, and then ride back into the hills. One night when it was kind of drizzling, Cousin John and Cousin Bill hitched their horses to the old rail in front of the little bar and went inside and played cards and got pretty reasonably drunk. About closing time, as they were going out the door, they noticed that the owner had put some cigars on a little counter near where you go out the door.

John stopped and said, "Cousin Bill, le's git us a seegar."

"John, don't care if I do."

So they both lit up and went out to get on their horses. John got up all right, but as Bill went to get on, his foot slipped and his mouth hit the side of the saddle and the cigar fell underneath the horse. He got down and felt around in the dark and finally found it, and wiped it off on his britches leg and stuck it in his mouth.

Then he made a buzzing and spitting sound with his mouth, and said, "Cousin John, did you ever taste of a seegar that had fell in the mud where the horses had been stompin' 'round?"

"No, Bill, why?" replied John.

"Well," said Bill, "I just want to tell you that you ain't missed nothin'."

North Carolinians who never knew Judge Alley, Sir Walter, or Justice Higgins, have missed plenty. Justice Higgins is not only known as the Blue Beard of the Blue Ridge, but in these modern times might well be called the Sputnick of Sparta. He told me one time that when he started to practice law, he had a little cubbyhole of an office in the courthouse at Sparta. One day when he was sitting at his typewriter, a mountain woman came to the door with an armful of papers, and looking over at him, said, "Young man, can you draw a deed?" He said he believed he could.

"There ain't nary other lawyer in town today," she said, "so I guess I'll have to use you. How much do you charge?"

"I charge $5.00," he told her.

"How long will it take you?"

"Oh, about five minutes."

"My Lord!" she exclaimed. "A dollar a minute to draw a deed? Well, there hain't nary other lawyer in town, so I guess you'll have to draw it. Here is these papers. Now git busy."

Justice Higgins was writing the deed when a friend came by and they chatted awhile. When a third party appeared on the scene, the old lady came over and tapped him on the shoulder. "Young man," she said, "If I'm a-gonna pay you a dollar a minute to draw me a deed, I don't want you to waste no time!"

Justice Higgins told me that up in Sparta, Cousin Bill used to get drunk and stay drunk, but that Cousin John would get on sprees with Bill but would sober up. They had been on a sort of protracted spree one time and were walking down the street arm-in-arm, when

John said, "Cousin Bill, it ain't this gettin' drunk that's so bad, as I see it. It's this gettin' sober that presents a problem to me."

Bill said, "Cousin John, I agree about that, and I have always tried to guard against just that kind of thing."

Sir Walter said he was always on guard against pessimism and grouchiness, and didn't waste any time with old R. E. Morse and Mr. Gloom.

CALL YOUR NEXT CASE.

27

SIR WALTER said that after hearing the hillbillies sing *John Henry,* he was convinced that John Henry was born in Chatham County. He said he was bound to have been born just northeast of the Devil's Trawmpin' Groun'. He claimed that if you would look close enough, you could see that Chatham County had the genuine counterpart of most every outstanding thing or person. *John Henry,* of course, is sort of like *St. Louis Blues.* It may get old, but it won't ever die out.

One of the beautiful things about Sir Walter that

kept him always fresh and exuberant was the fact that he kept up with everything from Einstein to jukeboxes. He would enjoy good old mountain folk songs one minute and Bach the next. All in between, he would see some humorous grounds of distraction, and predicted Elvis before he was born. He also said that a man named Schubert wrote a thing called a Serenade, but that some hillbillies were pushing him off the air with a song about trying to get some woman named Irene to go to bed. They played the song under his office window about 97 times and all they said was "Goodnight, Irene." The only way he got it stopped was to threaten the whole crowd with contempt of court. He said he was glad they were not singing *John Henry* because if they had been, it was doubtful that even a court contempt citation could have cooled them down.

In Wisconsin there once was a character of considerable portions known as John Paul Bunyan. He committed a lot of mighty deeds in the Northwest, but Sir Walter said that he was only a myth, and that the true great performer of such noble deeds of strength really lived in Chatham County, and his true name was Anderson Crutchfield. He lived over about Silk Hope. One day Anderson was plowing, and he had to go over into the next field and it was some distance to the gate. So Anderson Crutchfield just lifted up a twelve-hundred pound mule and set him on the other side of the fence. It is doubtful if this man Bunyan ever lived at all, but Anderson Crutchfield was born and raised in Chatham County, and walked to and fro in the flesh, and as Sir Walter would say, in his usual good style, "Many seed him and many knowed him."

Sir Walter often said that nothing could be better than to be born in Chatham County. He said that if a man could be born and raised in some of the rocky hillsides of Chatham and finally reach manhood, living in any other portion of the world would be like riding a bicycle downhill—easy. Many sturdy folks have come out of Chatham.

Weathering the financial storm known as Hurricane Hoover, was quite a feat. Most banks went down like the Titanic. It isn't any wonder that the smallest political gathering ever recorded in the history of this or any other country was a Hoover rally at Bishopville, South Carolina. At any rate, the Democrats grabbed hold of it and put Cleveland's Panic out of business for the Republicans. But the good old Chatham Bank in Siler City weathered the blow of the thirties, and the day that Franklin D. Roosevelt ordered the banks closed, J. J. Jenkins cussed him out and reported that he could pay his depositors 100 cents on the dollar. I asked Sir Walter why it was that this bank stood up so strong when all others seemed to be unable to open, and he gave his usual prompt and complete reply, by saying, "They just obeyed the banking laws." This grand old institution was organized in Chatham County in 1901. F. M. Hadley was president, L. L. Wren, vice-president, and J. J. Jenkins, cashier.

The men who are now operating the Chatham Bank, and some who have passed on, were good substantial solid citizens, and nothing keeps a bank liquid like having behind it some good solid citizens. The following is a list of these folks who have helped to make the history of Chatham Bank what it is now, and what it will be in the future: F. M. Hadley, J. J. Jenkins, J. C. Gregson, L. L. Wren, Daniel G. Fox, J. R. Parks, Dr. J. D. Edwards, J. N. Peoples, J. J. Johnson, J. T. Buckner, G. W. Perry, A. D. Lambe, William A. Teague, Wren, John T. Paschal, William R. Fox, James M. Jordan, C. Preston Fox, Curtis C. Brewer (now president), J. Lee Moody, H. Elton Stout, Frank G. Brooks, Dr. J. B. Earle, Ralph C. Self, William M. Wren (son of L. L. Wren, and left-handed golfer of considerable ability and my contemporary friend), W. B. Stamey, C. C. Brewer, Jr., P. M. Stewart, C. S. Gaines, A. W. Goldston, W. W. Burke, L. H. Smith, Jr., T. A. Johnson, V. H. Dameron, and Troy Smith.

Sir Walter told me that one time along in the year 1933, he was walking down the streets of Siler City and he heard some children talking. One said, "Let's play store." Another one said, "We can't. We ain't got any money." And another one said, "Well, then, let's play bank."

Depression or no depression, whether it be John Henry or Anderson Crutchfield, some sturdy folks have come from Chatham County. Some sturdy folks remain there, and unless the Lord returns soon, there will be many there when the rest of us are dead and gone on to the Glory Land.

CALL YOUR NEXT CASE.

28

SIR WALTER one time paid me a high compliment, saying to me, "Seawell, you have not only defended the docket and prosecuted the docket, but by the eternal, you have also been *on* the docket, and thereby have a great advantage over the average lawyer."

This was more truth than poetry, and while we think we know something about the administration of justice, we don't really appreciate it until we have been chosen to be administered upon. I had been a Referee in Bankruptcy under Judge Hayes for fourteen years and had handled some twenty million dollars in assets, but a government expert came down from Washington and said I was about eight thousand dollars short in my accounts. He had figured he had discovered another Teapot Dome, and called out everything but the Army. I knew it wasn't true, but that didn't keep it from being in headlines in all the daily papers.

It is in times like this when your true friends come to light. I will never forget passing through Pittsboro on the morning that the papers carried the headlines. My old friend Wade Barber, Sir Walter's law partner, was standing on the courthouse square as I drove around it, going toward Raleigh. He put his hand to his mouth and hollered, "I don't believe a word of it!"

I gave him a high-sign and hollered back, "I don't either!"

I saw Sir Walter over in Raleigh and he said, "Go get some lawyers, regardless of what the circumstances are, because a man who appears for himself usually has a fool for a client."

One of the most violent presumptions in circulation in this country is that the government is always right. Let's admit that it frequently is right. But they *do* make mistakes. The average lawyer may think that he knows something about the practice of law, but he really does not appreciate such "carryin's on" until he has been the defendant in a criminal suit.

About the time all this commotion got started, I was to introduce Governor Broughton to a District Meeting of Rotary at Wadesboro. He had already made inquiry as to whether anybody thought there was anything to the charges made against me, but when I got to Wadesboro, he called me off by myself and asked me personally if there was anything to it. I said, "Governor, they most likely will hang me on the back side of the courthouse in Greensboro early some Sunday morning."

"That is exactly what I thought," he said, and from then on we just enjoyed the situation. Somebody said one time that it is really not necessary to explain anything, because your enemies won't believe you and your friends don't require it.

Among a multitude that showed up before trial, was my friend Judge Frank Armstrong, of Troy. He wired me the day before trial and the day the trial started, and as Huck Finn said about Tom Sawyer, "He war my friend and I ain't forgot it." After the trial was over, Judge E. Yates Webb wrote me a fine letter and I ain't forgot that either. He and his brother, James E. Webb, are two of the finest men North Carolina ever produced. Judge Varser, Clyde Douglass and Roy McMillan appeared for me, and we went down and listened to what the government had to offer, and when they finished all they had to offer, Judge Webb kicked the whole thing out of court. Everybody shook hands and congratulated everybody and said how much they enjoyed the trial. The newspaper folks thanked me because I didn't cuss them out about printing everything and taking pictures, and then the Judge came out and thanked everybody all over again and we had a sort of fellowship meeting in the courtroom. I was sorry that Judge Hayes wasn't there because when all this fuss started, they sort of staked him out and fixed it so he couldn't even see me without them trying to put something on him. However, he wrote me a mighty good letter. Of course, after the trial I got a multitude of letters from people all over the state, saying they "knowed it all the time."

There is nothing in this world can take the place of experience. I know that I am not the only lawyer who has ever been tried, but Sir Walter was right when he said any lawyer who has been tried has an advantage over one who hasn't. It is like being operated on for appendicitis—it won't do you any good to let the doctor take out somebody else's. He has to take out yours.

No matter what happened, Sir Walter could see the humorous side of whatever was in the wind. He used to send me clippings from the paper just about every day. One day I got this headline clipping: JAPS CAPTURE WAKE ISLAND—SEAWELL UNDER FIRE. After the case was over, Sir Walter wrote me and said that he hoped that now that the government had lost the battle on the home front they would get busy on the foreign front with an enemy that was important and really amounted to something.

Shortly after this, rationing set in and travel got down to a minimum, and getting from Carthage to Pittsboro was like going from Raleigh to Richmond. Things got mighty confusing along about this time, but somehow or other, between Hadacol and Lydia Pinkhams compound, we made it. (*It is peculiar how folks will give the glory to everything in the world except the Lord.*)

A few weeks after court, some man asked me how many lawyers I had at the trial. I told him four. He said he hadn't seen but three. I told him I had one there that you can see only by faith. You can't see Him with your naked fleshly eye. The man looked at me kind of sad and pitiful-like, just like folks do that do not know the Lord, and especially when they think that you are going to testify to them about the Lord Jesus Christ and His saving Grace. Or maybe they think you are going to come right out flatfooted and ask them if they are saved. Then when they leave you and talk about you to other folks, they will say, "He is a good fellow all right, but he has gone kind of crazy on religion."

The natural man receiveth not the things of the Spirit of God, they are foolishness unto him, neither can he know them because they are Spiritually discerned.

CALL YOUR NEXT CASE.

29

SIR WALTER was first called "Sir Walter" by Chief Justice Walter P. Stacy of the North Carolina Supreme Court, according to my best recollection. We had arrived in Raleigh one morning when court was not in session, and Sir Walter led the way to the office of the Chief Justice. As we entered, Sir Walter bowed low and said, "Good morning, My Lord, *sic semper tyrannis.*"

The Chief Justice got up from his seat behind his big mahogany desk, and putting out his hand, said, "Good morning, Sir Walter. I am delighted to see you."

185

That "Sir Walter" business stuck in my mind. I can prove by Adrian Newton, the Supreme Court clerk at this writing, and get it backed up by the marshal, my old friend Dillard Gardner, that this was a genuine Judge Walter Siler greeting, especially that "sic semper tyrannis" part, although he had other Latin for other occasions.

After the Chief Justice and Sir Walter spent a few minutes in special greetings to each other, they would finally observe that I was present too, and we would sort of begin the whole thing all over again. The Chief Justice was mighty nice to me as a young lawyer, but then I am sure he was always nice to all the young lawyers because that was just his natural way.

Usually, before we could get out of the office of the Chief Justice, other Justices would come in and usually it was Justice double A. F. Seawell, father of Judge Malcolm Seawell, the present attorney general of North Carolina. Justice Seawell always wanted to tell his favorite joke about the do-do bird that always flew backwards, because he didn't give a tinker's damn about where he was going, but he did want to see where he had been. He also loved to tell about old Captain Swift Galloway walking up the street in Snow Hill and meeting some citizen, and the citizen saying, "Mr. Swift, how is everything?"

And Captain Galloway would say, "They're gaining on us. By golly, they are about to overtake us."

And then the citizen would ask, "Who?"

And he would answer, "The S.O.B.'s!"

At the office of the Chief Justice we would also usually meet Justice Schenk, Justice Devin, and Justice Winborne, who is now Chief Justice. Justice Devin became Chief Justice after the death of Justice Stacy. To listen to these men was indeed a sort of liberal education in itself. It helped me in many ways in the practice of law and fixed it so I could avoid many a pitfall.

I found out that judges are nothing but human beings doing the best they can to try to remember what the law is and how to apply it to the facts. Most of the time the judge is just as scared as you are, and almost as scared as the defendants.

This reminds me of what Judge Rousseau told on himself. He was holding court at Wentworth and after court he wanted to go over to Reidsville to spend the night. He drove down to a corner and saw a policeman and asked him how to get to Reidsville. The officer told him to go to the cloverleaf intersection and take a certain turn and come under the road at the overhead bridge, and that would take him right into Reidsville. The Judge did like he thought the officer told him, but each time came right back where he started from. So, not realizing that it was the same man he had asked earlier, he went up to a policeman and said, "Mr. Officer, can you tell me how to get from Wentworth to Reidsville?"

The officer looked at him kind of casual-like, and said, "Well, I will tell you again, but damn if I believe you got sense enough to get to Reidsville."

The Judge said, "Well, Mr. Officer, that may be so,

but I have to hold court here tomorrow, and I want to go over to Reidsville and get some rest tonight."

The officer jumped back and said, "Good gosh! Is this Judge Rousseau? Please forgive me, Judge. I didn't know it was you. I got cases before you tomorrow. Please, Judge, don't say nothin' about this."

The Judge looked him right in the eye and said, "Mr. Officer, if you won't say anything about this, I sure won't. Let's *both* keep this thing a secret."

I was in court at Carthage one day and Judge Rousseau was on the bench, and he called a divorce case where I represented the plaintiff. The plaintiff was not in the courtroom at the time and I got up and said, "If Your Honor pleases, my client was here just a minute ago."

Judge Rousseau said, "Mr. Seawell, we didn't want him a minute ago. The question is, where is he *now?*"

"If Your Honor please," I replied, "I saw my client right under the oak tree on the courthouse lawn just a minute ago."

Judge Rousseau stared straight at me for a moment. Then he said, "Don't you reckon what your client wants us to do is give him *curb service?*"

The time *may* come when we *will* have drive-in courthouses. We have most everything else in that category now, including drive-in banks, churches, and theaters. However, it is doubtful if we will ever be able to administer justice as you would operate a supermarket. Such a procedure would be just one step closer to complete Communism.

Sir Walter said that when he had a case of some significance, he usually went down to Sanford and gave the facts to A. A. F. Seawell, because he didn't have to look up the law, but could tell you what it was right out of his head. After A. A. F. Seawell would collaborate with Sir Walter some on the law, he would then go over to see K. R. Hoyle and get him to do the work, because he was the workin'est lawyer in the entire jurisdiction. K. R. Hoyle was the senior member of the firm of Hoyle & Hoyle in Sanford, N. C. There is also another firm of Hoyle & Hoyle in Greensboro, which is also a root out of the same branch of Hoyles. Somebody said one time that law firms may come and law firms may go, but Hoyle & Hoyle goes on forever. Senator Jim Hoyle and Solicitor Dick Hoyle are stepping in their father's footprints, but it is doubtful if both of them put together will ever do as much work as their father, K. R. Hoyle—although they are making a good effort, and might succeed.

K. R. Hoyle told Sir Walter one time that if the Supreme Court did not reverse a certain judge in a judgment entered, he would throw his license to practice out the window and quit. In the particular case, he took 269 exceptions. After arguing and waiting for some time to hear from the Supreme Court, the Supreme Court affirmed the lower court by a per curiam opinion, which, of course, was no opinion at all. So Mr. Hoyle observed that he "knew darn well" they could not write an opinion in that case without reversing the lower court. Sir Walter said that a per curiam opinion was the same thing to the Supreme Court as a snorkel is to a submarine—it lets them breath without being apprehended.

Of course, there is a difference in judges, and the kind of imprint they make on the public. Sir Walter said he had a man drive him to two courts one day, and he and his driver spent half a day at one courthouse and half a day at the other. On the way home he asked the colored driver what he thought of the courts that day, and Sir Walter got this reply: "I had rather be found guilty in Mr. Judge Gwyn's court, than to be found not guilty in Mr. Judge Hunt Parker's court."

In all courts there is that human element that gets into the procedure and there is nothing you can do about it, because no two men are alike, no matter how well versed they may be in the knowledge of the law. I have often enjoyed listening to Sir Walter and other judges and lawyers discussing the lawyers of North Carolina, and actually they remind you of members of some large family. From Poisson at Wilmington to Van Winkle at Asheville, and from Judge Chester Morris at Coinjack to Judge George Patton at Franklin, and all throughout the great state of North Carolina, the lawyers seem to me like one great family of folks.

As a little boy, I used to sit in the lap of Judge Henry Groves Connor and hear him tell some interesting court story, and then I remember Judge W. S. O'B. Robinson and how he and my father used to have such a rollickin' good time when they were together. They told one time how Judge Robinson used to put cotton in his ears when the lawyers got to speaking too loud, and it got in the newspapers and made the Judge kind of mad. One day a lawyer at Carthage was ripping the roof off the courthouse with a speech and Judge Robinson called my father to the bench and asked him if he knew any way he could stop the noise. My father replied, "Judge, cotton is only five cents a pound." This got him so tickled that the lawyer's yelling became unimportant.

Hambone said in his meditations, "A lawyer advises you, but a judge tells you what you are gonna do." Of course, people in the toils of the law have been known to just throw themselves on the ignorance of the court, and sometimes it works.

CALL YOUR NEXT CASE.

30

SIR WALTER said that after reading the record and becoming familiar with the facts and the general reports involved, he had come to the conclusion that George Washington couldn't tell a lie, Joseph Stalin couldn't tell the truth, and Harry Truman could not tell the difference. He would often repeat the statement that Missouri was the greatest state in the Union because it gave Jesse James and Harry Truman to the nation. I was positive, however, that Sir Walter voted for Truman, because Tom Dewey was utterly distasteful to him, especially after his campaign chairman, Herbert Brownell, announced in August that

Dewey was elected, though the election was not until November.

The best time to announce an election is after it is over with. "We will win" is a good slogan, but "We have won" is in bad taste, and helps gets votes for the other man. After the election in 1948, Sir Walter said he had a lot more respect for Mr. Truman, even if he did have a lot of un-southerly manners. He said that although Mr. Truman was a sort of semi-southerner, he had been in Washington too long, had become contaminated with the do-gooders and the integraters, and was completely un-flavorful to the Dixiecrats.

The Dixiecrats made a good showing in some places, but everybody who sings, "I wish I was in Dixie" does not necessarily know anything about Dixie, and is usually just singing to be singing and doesn't have much heart in it. Sort of like the oldtime solicitor, John Queen, who refused to prosecute a man for impersonating a woman's husband. He said, "If it pleases Your Honor, this man and his wife and this other man got themselves a half-gallon of liquor and proceeded to get drunk together and cause untold confusion among themselves, and as for the prosecution of this case, my heart just ain't in it." Usually it is mighty hard for a man to call himself a Dixiecrat after having fought the battles of the Democrats for so many years, and his heart just won't be in it.

The last campaign that Sir Walter had any part in was the one in 1948. He said he was about in distress however, because he had no taste for Dewey, and he had

lost his taste for Truman. But Kerr Scott had added a
portion of pepper and other flavor to the situation in
North Carolina, so he said he would stick it out with
the regulars. He said that when Scott got to Washington and could have his way about most things up there,
he would most likely plow Washington under, and
plant it in lespedeza. He also said there was no danger
of any of our enemies from abroad ever dropping any
kind of bomb on Washington because it was the seat
of all our international, to say nothing of local, confusion.

We often talked about the predicament of politics in
the South. Both major political parties have by-passed
the South. We agreed that if the South ever loses its
seniority with respect to U. S. Senators and Congress-
men, we might just as well be a foreign country, so far
as any voice in the nation is concerned. Then we could
just send representatives to the United Nations, put
everything down South in the Foreign Aid program,
get in on the Marshall Plan and go back to shooting
Revenue Officers. What most political leaders don't
understand is that they don't understand the South. We
have a peculiar situation down here that is foreign to
any other situation in the world. These situations vary
even from county to county and so government in the
South must be local and run by local folks. Shakespeare
said that you can't make a silk purse out of a sow's ear,
but, according to Sir Walter, you can make a sow's ear
out of a silk purse, if you handle it right. Tyranny
appears many times in the robe of reform, progress,

enlightment, special services and humanitarian rights.

Sir Walter often said that many a man in this country would give up the right of habeas corpus and other rights under the Constitution, if he thought that the Government would pay his hospital bill. While it is true that Sir Walter enjoyed his politics, he was serious enough when necessary, to understand that being too serious was sometimes fatal. Speaking to the Rotary Club of High Point on May 13, 1948, Sir Walter made a strong appeal for Ola Ray Boyd for Governor and said among other things:

"I have spent much of my life pounding away at the imprisoned twelve in the jury box, or extolling the angelic perfections of one political party and recounting the manifold shortcomings of the other, and I have developed considerable lung power along these lines. But today I want to call to your attention a magnificent spectacle now taking place in our wonderful State of North Carolina. Not since the days of ancient Rome and her chariot races, has civilization seen such a demonstration of magnificence. The Gubernatorial Marathon is now on. Visualize the scene. Whizzing down the course in his housetrailer comes Governor Albright; close on his heels comes Governor Barker and his school bus; then in the review comes Kerr Scott, strutting along on his farm-all tractor; and up rides Governor Johnson on his motorcycle, carrying a banner saying, 'We have an eighty million dollar surplus.' As he passes by, he raises another banner, saying 'Let's issue a hundred million dollars in new bonds.'

"This makes a beautiful setting, but my purpose here today is to point out to you one on the racetrack that you may not have observed. Men may cry peace; teachers may cry for salary bonus; employees may cry for a raise in compensation; housewives may cry for cessation of meatless Mondays, sugarless Saturdays and cookless Sundays; C. I. O. organizers may cry for more wages and less work; ardent drys may cry for liquor referendums; dripping wets may cry for bigger and more abundant liquor stores; babies may cry for Castoria; but I cry unto you in stentorian tones that the emergency of the situation and the situation of the emergency demand that we listen to the call of that son of the soil, that potent pork producer, that patriotic pig producer and hog caller of Carolina—none other than Ola Ray Boyd of Pinetown, Beaufort County."

Sir Walter never took his politics too seriously, and he often advised me along the same line, and this is good advice. Nevertheless, you often meet folks who will say that you have a right to your opinions about matters just so long as they agree with theirs, and some of the simple-minded will almost insult you over some political notion which may be contrary to their notions.

Of course, being a Republican down South is like working for your board and losing your appetite. Also when you run on the Republican ticket in the South you usually come under that old Persian proverb which says, "Blessed is he that expecteth nothing, for he shall not be disappointed." The trouble with politics is that it has the element of human nature in it and that makes it bad, unless you understand it, and recognize it, and ignore it.

Sir Walter said that a man named Lewis who had pink whiskers was running for Congress one time, and his enemies began telling a multitude of lies on him, and his campaign managers came to him and asked what he intended to do about those lies. He said to ignore every one of them—they didn't amount to anything since they were just lies. Finally they came to him and said, "They are now telling that you are a terrible man to run after women, and you are crazy about women."

"Well now," said Mr. Lewis, "that has some element of truth in it, and we had better deny it at once."

All the Superior Court judges in North Carolina are Democrats and it has been this way for many years, and they, of course, are all interested in politics. But in spite of this political flavor, we have a magnificent bench in this state. Sir Walter said that one of his favorite judges of the Superior Court was Judge Henry Stevens of Warsaw. He said he was not only a good judge, but he just overflowed with human nature. Before Judge Stevens became Superior Court judge, he was National Commander of the American Legion, which is about as much honor as being President of the United States, without all the cussing and disgrace that goes with it.

One time Judge Stevens was holding court in the old courthouse at Hillsboro. It had the same furniture in it that Cornwallis used when he was there, and some of it

was second-hand then, having been brought up from
New Bern by Daniel Boone or Richard Dobbs Spaight
or somebody like that. When Judge Stevens sat down
in the chair of the bench, it cracked and almost threw
him to the floor. After court got started, one of the
jurors leaned back in his chair and it popped like a
pistol and spilled the juror out on the floor and col-
lapsed in every direction. Judge Stevens jumped to his
feet and shouted, "Mr. Juror, did you get hurt? I hope
if you did that you will sue this dad-burned county for
a hundred thousand dollars!"

Today, one of the most beautiful courtrooms in
North Carolina is at Hillsboro. They have a handsome
judge's bench and sturdy, very comfortable mahogany
chairs. They have put up a lot of plaques around the
courthouse about people who did this and who did
that, but in my opinion, it was Judge Henry Stevens
who should have a plaque for having got the new building idea in circulation.

Sir Walter said that some folks will run for public
office when they haven't any more chance of getting
elected than Senator Tom Heflin would have had of
becoming Pope. Sir Walter said the way the running
fever usually gets started is for some man to be asked to
speak at the Rotary, the Kiwanis, the Lions, the Bears,
the Elks, or some so-called service club. This is an invi-
tation for him to file at once for governor. As soon as
these runners get started they immediately come out
for increased government services and lower taxes. This
is a good kind of a campaign lie and everybody knows

that it is a lie but just the same they love to listen to it. It sounds good, and they like to listen to it. However, politics mixed in with human nature makes quite a mixture, and anything can happen. It is somewhat like the colored man who said he didn't preach, he just exhorted. When asked what was the difference between exhorting and preaching, he said that when a man preaches, he has to stick to his text. But when a man exhorts, he can branch off in all directions.

Sir Walter said that the greatest politician this country had ever seen or ever would see was Franklin D. Roosevelt. Shortly after Mr. Roosevelt died, claimed Sir Walter, a hillbilly was singing a song dedicated to Mr. Roosevelt. It was called, "I Dreamed I Searched Heaven For You." Some old mossback Republican spoke up and said, "Hit shore must have been a dream all right, because you was searchin' in the wrong place."

CALL YOUR NEXT CASE.

31

SIR WALTER, many times referred to as the Sage of Siler City, loved the southern accent. I spoke one time to an educational group, and my subject was "The Simplicity of Ignorance." At the conclusion, a very charming lady presented me with a copy of the book by my old friend, William T. Polk, entitled, *Southern Accent.* ~~There is a certain kind~~ of peculiar romance about the South that sort of grips everybody in the South, and even when Yankees come down and visit us, it gets in their blood, and if you don't watch them close, they will go home and write some sort of a book like they had made some big discovery about something in the South.

Sir Walter loved to write little sketches about great leaders in the South, and he would have had a great deal in common with Burke Davis, the great southern Civil War serenader. Sir Walter and Mr. Davis, singing a song together about the virtues and noble heart of Robert E. Lee, would have been a cloud moving. Of course, things have changed considerable since the days of Lee, Jackson and Jeb Stuart, and nowadays if anyone joins any organization dedicated to the overthrow of the government by force and violence, those in charge get awful mad and they will indict you and put you in the federal prison or they might even hang you. It isn't so much what you do, but how you do it. If your technique is good, they might put you up a monument and call you a hero. I had five great-uncles who tried to overthrow the government one time by force and violence, and they did pretty good until they struck Gettysburg. They made such a noble effort that the taxpayers erected a monument to them. Most folks are not qualified to overthrow the government, even at the ballot box.

When I think about that word "qualified," I am reminded of what happened one time in the practice of law back in the thirties when Sir Walter and I used to get together and talk over our different uses of technique in the everyday practice of the law. One time we collected out of the Seaboard Railroad for killing a cow between Cameron and Southern Pines because *a bull*

*got run over on the Atlantic and Yadkin Railroad
between Siler City and Greensboro.* Now, you really
have to know your technique when you get into a situation like this. I wrote to the Seaboard and demanded
pay for the cow and they wrote right back and said that
North Carolina had a stock law and that the cow had
no business being loose.

I wrote back and said they didn't ring the bell and
blow the whistle, and they wrote right back and said
they didn't have to ring the bell and blow the whistle,
that the cow should have remained tied or inside a
fence, and they said they wouldn' pay a cent, much less
the $100 I was demanding for the cow. I finally made
one desperate effort and wrote and asked them to pay
the $100, and I said, "I am making this demand just
like the man who had his bull run over by the Atlantic
& Yadkin railroad between Siler City and Greensboro"
and that I was giving them the letter verbatim et punc-
tuatim, in words and figgers as follows:

"Mr. ———, A & Y Raleroad
Greensboro, N. C.
Dear kind frend and sir:

last Wensy I think it war your raleroad runned
over my bull at the forty mile pass. He air not dade
but mought as well be. Hit skint him from the tip
of his horns to the tip of his tale and it taken a
patch outen his belly to the squar of a yard. He
war a red bull and he now stand aroun in the barn
yard and he look awful blue. He air too tough for

beef, he air too broke up to be a oxen, and he air
now wholy unqualerfide to be a bull. Please mark
him dead and paid fer and send me forty dollars.
                                    Yours truly."

In a few days I got a letter back and it went something like this:

Dear kind friend and Sir:

We don't owe you anything for the cow, we never
intend to pay you one cent for the cow, you may as
well quit writing to us about the cow because we
never expect to ever pay you one cent for the cow;
BUT, we think that the BULL LETTER is worth
at least a hundred dollars and our check is here-
with enclosed."

This proves that in spite of what some folks say about
cold-blooded corporations, if you tap in the right place
you can usually find some soul close around who has a
sense of humor and considerable kindly feelings in his
heart.

Technique, of course, is a sort of outgrowth of auto-
matic diplomacy circumscribed and completely surrounded by common sense. Sir Walter used to love to
tell about the man who came to him about trouble he
was having with his wife. He employed Sir Walter to
try to see if he couldn't get his wife to take him back
into her good graces. Sir Walter told his client to let
him in on a few secrets of his married life and to promise him that he wouldn't get mad no matter what was

said. The client promised, and so when the man's wife went on the stand, Sir Walter began to say all kinds of things calculated to make her mad. He finally moved his chair up close and kept poking his finger right under the woman's nose and making all kinds of insinuating remarks. At last she said, "Walter Siler, if you would keep your big mouth out of this, me and John could run our affairs all right!"

Sir Walter bowed real low and said, "Madam, take over," and according to the record, they lived happily ever after and had six children born at their house.

Of course, sometimes folks hand out what is called a lefthanded item of forgiveness, sort of like saying that so-and-so is a very lovely person in a repulsive sort of way. Which brings to mind what Vernon Patterson told me about the colored preacher who got up in the pulpit to preach and a little dog came up close to him in the pulpit and began to rub up against his leg. The preacher sort of pushed the little dog aside with his foot, but he came right back, and after he had pushed him aside about three times, he hauled off and kicked him right in the center and the little dog yelped and ran out of the church down the middle aisle.

After the sermon one of the deacons met the preacher out in the yard where the crowd was milling about. "Preacher," he said, "you done near 'bout ruined yourself at this church. That dog you kicked was Deacon Jones' dog and he is one of the best contributors we got at this church. You better look him up right now and 'pologize."

The preacher said, "I shore will do that right now. I don't want no trouble with Deacon Jones." When he found him in the churchyard, he said, "Deacon Jones, I didn't know that was your little dog I kicked. He's a right pretty little dog and I wouldn't of kicked him under no circumstances if I had just a-knowed it was your dog."

"Oh," replied the deacon, "dat's all right, Preacher. I'm glad you kicked that dog outen the church. I didn't want him to hear that sermon nohow."

Since I began to jot these things down, several whose names appear in stories or experiences in this book have passed away. I think particularly of Judge John J. Parker, Judge W. A. Leland McKeithan, Senator Kerr Scott and Judge J. A. Rousseau. Judge Parker had reached his three score years and ten, but Judge McKeithan was just getting to that place where he was rendering great service to the state and nation, and had an expectancy of many more years. Senator Scott and Judge Rousseau still had several years to go, according to the time usually allotted by the Lord. So sudden was the leaving of these distinguished North Carolinians that it is hard to realize that they are gone.

A noted atheist said one time that life was the small thread of light that existed between the cold and barren peaks of two eternities. That we cried aloud, but the only reply was the echo of our wailing cry, but that in the sad hour of death Hope saw a Star and listening Love could hear the rustle of a wing. They are pretty words but nothing in them, no comfort. In the sad hour of death, if the Lord tarry, I want to hear the words of the Creator when He said, while He journeyed here in the flesh, *"I am the resurrection and the life, whosoever believeth in me though he were dead yet shall he live, and whosoever liveth and believeth in me shall never die."*

I was with my old friend Redd Harper on a speaking trip down in Georgia a few years ago. Redd is the man who played "Mr. Texas" in the Billy Graham movies, *Oil Town* and *Mr. Texas,* and is one of the great soul winners of this modern day. As we walked into one of the chapels at the R. G. LeTourneau factory, there was a sign up over the door which read: "Life is short. It will soon be passed. Only what is done for Christ will last." Redd looked at me and said, "Guv, the Gospel is such a simple message that many folks stumble all over it and won't believe. Nevertheless, the power is in the *Word* and not in us, and all we can do is just give it out."

Moreover brethren, I declare unto you the Gospel, how that Christ died for our sins, according to the Scriptures.

CALL YOUR NEXT CASE.

32

SIR WALTER departed this life Sunday morning, February 11, 1951, and went on over into the glory land. When I got the news I felt mighty sad and melancholy, and then I got to thinking what he said one time about being sad and melancholy, and it cheered me up considerable. He said that the saddest time he ever experienced outside being in the presence of death, was his memories of the old days along about 1912 up in Siler City. He said he used to sit on the porch on Sunday afternoon in the summertime along about five o'clock. All you could hear was the drone of a few flies, 'most too lazy to fly in the hot afternoon atmosphere. Down in the valley you could hear the tinkle of a cowbell, and the way it was tinkling you could tell she was lying down. Off in the woods you could hear the mournful sound of a raincrow, broadcasting about every ten minutes; and then the wind would cause a little shuffle of the bushes at the edge of the porch and way over on Deep River you could hear the rumble of thunder. And all this caused you to feel awful sad and melancholy, and just about the time you thought you would shed a few tears over nothing at all, a dogfight would break out down the street and in a minute or two it would sound like Hell had laid an egg. Then it would get quiet again and somebody would holler across the street and say, "Do you reckon it's gonna rain?" This sort of fetched everything back to normalcy again, and you would get over that real blue feeling and begin to think about eating another piece of that Sunday cake that had given you the indigestion so bad you couldn't sleep all that afternoon.

Sir Walter was a member of the Hickory Mountain Methodist Church. His funeral was preached in the First Methodist Church in Siler City. In charge was The Reverend E. R. Clegg, assisted by The Reverend W. A. Seawell of the Hickory Mountain Methodist Church, and his long-time friend and law partner, that lovable old bluestocking Presbyterian, Wade Barber, of Pittsboro. Active pallbearers at the funeral were Thomas Wren, William Wren, William Reid Thompson, Buster Edwards, Lloyd Womble and Lynton

Womble. The honorary pallbearers were T. Fleet Baldwin, L. P. Dixon, R. F. Paschal, Congressman Harold D. Cooley, E. L. Gavin and Robert L. Gavin. I believe that every newspaper in North Carolina had something to say about the passing of Judge Siler.

The Greensboro Daily News reported: "Death of Walter D. Siler, 72, Sunday at his home in Siler City did not come as a shock to those who knew him best and most keenly appreciated this man of proven capacity as legislator, trial lawyer, solicitor and Judge of both County and Superior Courts. He has been ill for three years, but had the Grim Reaper come to him in the midst of a trial over which he was presiding or in which he was prosecuting a defendant or representing a client, Walter Siler would have taken his enforced exit in stride. For his chief characteristic was a sense of proportion which never let him take himself too seriously. As a solicitor he was vigorous; as a Judge, fair; as a commentator on current affairs, a trifle caustic, but never self-righteous. 'A fellow of infinite jest' Shakespeare had Hamlet say of Yorick. So was Walter Siler, but he would never have been a death's head, even if he had been forced to listen to his friend's soliloquy. He had no question of to be or not to be—he simply was a good man of his mental hands, and charming company for those who refused to get gummed up with or by frustration."

Sir Walter was buried in the shade of the ancient cedar trees of the old Presbyterian Cemetery in Pittsboro. When I pass this cemetery and see the old trees and look on the quiet scene, I think of the poem that John Charles McNeill wrote about an old friend of his. This starts that old and melancholy feeling. Of course, if John Charles McNeill had lived to this present time and would write his famous poems about the colored brethren now as he did then, he would most likely be indicted. No poet who ever lived in North Carolina could quite touch the human heartstrings like John Charles McNeill. He also had a significant sense of humor, and this is set forth in his books *Songs Merry and Sad* and *Lyrics from Cotton Land*. So, with apologies to John Charles McNeill, I write this little sketch about Sir Walter buried in the shade of the old cedar trees in the Presbyterian Cemetery at Pittsboro:

> The cedar berries cluster blue
> The cedar birds are gay
> Amid the bossie boughs that shade
> The old man's dust today.
>
> He knows no times and seasons now
> No need to call the Tiler
> No change of jurisdiction now
> For my old friend, Judge Siler.

While Sir Walter was sick, I went to see him several times and had high hopes that he would recover from the slight stroke which he had suffered. He was a great admirer of Abraham Lincoln and came pretty close to dying on his birthday.

It would have been a great joy and pleasure to me if Sir Walter could have lived long enough to have seen me running for Governor of North Carolina on the

Republican ticket and introducing Ike and Mamie around over the State. What he would have said about me cavorting with foreigners under such circumstances would have been a joy to hear. Truly General Eisenhower was as charming as any man you would want to meet and Mrs. Eisenhower likewise, but after the election, the Sanhedrin of the Progressive Republicans boxed Ike off into a secret place behind the nylon curtain and made a sort of tin god idol out of him, refused to let him lead, and used him for election purposes only. Due to this boxed-in situation President Eisenhower was not permitted to lead the people like Roosevelt and he also lacked the aggressiveness of Truman. So the Republican Royal Guard made a sort of "ark of the covenant" out of him and toted him around in the wilderness and Red Sea of Farm Relief and Foreign Policy, and it worked well. When you meet Ike and feel his warm handshake and see him smile all the way across his face from ear to ear, you can almost forget he is a Republican. Truman knew exactly what he was doing when he asked him to run on the Democratic ticket.

What most folks don't know in this country today is that we are no longer a democracy. We are a super-saturated solution of socialism. We are a socialized republic. If Eugene V. Debs could rise from the dead and come back here now, he would be too embarrassed to join either party as they have both gone too far to the left. We will most likely keep on having elections, but as for our form of government, it is fixed in socialism and the people like it, and multitudes are looking for that day when they can reach the age where they can "re-tarr."

Sir Walter was well grounded in political science and no man knew the southern people any better than he did. He told me about a traveling salesman who was trying to cross Georgia one time on Primary Day. The whole state was in a political stew. Word got out that this man was a Democrat, and they voted him eight times before he could get across the state line.

A short time ago the *News and Observer* called me and asked me if I had any political plans for the future, and a story of Sir Walter's came to my mind. It was about a man who was found dead on the banks of the Yadkin River one cold January day several years ago. A coroner's jury investigated and they made their return as follows: "We this here coroners jury, find that this here man was hit in the head and killed, he was throwed in the river and drowned, and he was washed up on the shore and froze to death, and he air now dade."

Being politically dead helps to give one a better vision both "back'ards" and "for'ards." The year 1916 is as far back as I can remember in politics. At that time the slogan was "Vote for Wilson and Peace or Hughes and War," so everybody voted for Wilson, and in about six months war broke out. Then in 1920 everybody said, "Back to Normalcy" with Harding, and everybody voted for Harding, and nothing has been normal since. Then in 1924 along came Coolidge and he said that the country as a whole was prosperous, and he just laid the ground floor for Hoover. Then along came Hoover, who offered "Prohibition and Prosperity," and everybody voted for Hoover and he hadn't been in a year before everybody was flat broke and dead drunk.

Soon, along came Roosevelt and said, "I het waar," and we ain't had nothin' but "waar" ever since. Then along came Truman and he said he was "going out and give 'em hell" and he was right. Finally, along comes Ike and he says what this country needs is a balanced budget and a firm foreign policy, and soon as he gets in he says that it is impossible to balance the budget and nobody knows what in the world our foreign policy is.

When the Democrats were in office we had boondoggling and pump-priming and now that the Republicans are in, we have moondoggling and skyrocketing. The Republicans have now appointed an Administrator of Space. If Franklin D. Roosevelt could have lived long enough to make this appointment, the Republicans never would have gotten into office ever again. It will take at least three million lawyers to find out where space begins and where it ends. If people are given space lots and then they should get torn all to pieces by Haley's Comet, and left kneedeep in stardust and strewn with moonbeams, then they can put their lots in the Space Bank. The Soil Bank we have now ain't a circumstance. After we get the Space Bank going good, we can forget about the ceiling on the national debt because the sky will be the limit.

Sir Walter used to talk about people committing ambush on themselves. He should see what we are doing now. If this world is now being run by all the highly educated and intelligent brains that we can muster, why is it that we are in such a state of confusion? Is it not a lack of faith? Are people of ordinary simple faith and common sense unqualified for leadership?

According to Sir Walter, one of the sorriest exhibitions was to see some person basking in the sunlight of his own unimportance or sunning himself on the sands of his self-righteous conceit. There was a time in my life when I considered myself to be a very smart man. I remember that I took the North Carolina Supreme Court examination to practice law before I was 21 years old and had to wait around three or four months for adult status before I could be sworn in so I could practice law. Then I argued my first case in the Supreme Court of North Carolina when I was 22 (*State vs. Maness,* 192 N. C., page 708.), and they decided in my favor. Now at that time I would have made a voluntary affidavit that I knew more law than any man from Moses on down to Chief Justice Taft, and I thought that a man that smart should have a philosophy for himself, so I got me one up. I declared that I believed in doing right because right was right and not because of any promise or reward or fear of hell in the future, and I thought that that sounded pretty big.

I can remember when we used to meet at different places and attend what we called a soiree. We usually started off with a cocktail. A cocktail is the devil's name for a drink of liquor. Some folks won't take a drink of liquor, but most everybody will take a cocktail. Then we used always to want to talk about some new thing, and quote Bob Ingersoll and Tom Payne and look up and see what old George Bernard Shaw had to say over in England. We considered ourselves to belong to the intelligentsia or the highbrows. Now a highbrow is a man that has more education than his intelligence can stand. Nearly always, at these soirees, there would be present some young man with a baritone voice and he would want to sing "Invictus." Something about "Dark is the hole from Pole to Pole" and "Whatever gods there may be, I am the Captain of my soul," I think it went. "My head is bloody but unbowed," was also part of the boast.

And we were about the most self-righteous group you could come in contact with under any circumstances. Then one day I picked up my Bible and happened to turn to this verse: "Beware, lest any man spoil you through philosophy and vain deceit, after the tradition of men, after the rudiments of the world, and not after Christ." And then I turned to another place which said: "Trust in the Lord with all your heart and lean not to your own understanding, in all your ways acknowledge Him and He will direct your paths."

There was another verse: "The fear of the Lord is the beginning of wisdom." And then another: "The word of the Lord is Right."

And I shall never forget these words: "God, who in many parts and in many ways in times past spoke unto the fathers by the prophets, has in these last days spoken unto us in His Son, whom He hath appointed heir of all things, by whom also He planned the ages, who is the forthshining of His glory and the express image of His being and upholding all things by the word of His power, when He had by Himself purged our sins, sat down at the right hand of the majesty on high . . . for *by Him* were all things created that are in heaven and in earth, visible and invisible, whether they be thrones, dominions, principalities or powers, all things were created by Him and for Him and He is before all things and by Him all things consist, and He is the head of the body, the Church, who is the beginning, the first born out from among the dead that in all things He might have the preeminence, for it pleased the Father that in Him should all fullness dwell; and having made peace by the blood of His cross, by Him to reconcile all things unto Himself *by Him* I say, whether they be things in earth or things in heaven."

If any man will just confess his sins and conceit and kneel down at the Cross and ask Jesus Christ to save him, He'll do it. I don't understand it. It is a miracle. The wind bloweth and we hear the sound thereof, but we know not from whence it cometh or whither it goeth, so is every man born of the Spirit.

Sir Walter used to tell me that he loved everybody in North Carolina, and I used to tell him that I had my doubts about it, and then he said he had his doubts about it too, but it was a good thing to say because it wasn't likely to make anybody mad. Then Sir Walter used to love to talk about North Carolinians, and he used to do some considerable talking about Henry Jerome Stockard, a great poet and Chatham County's contribution to the literary world. This man wrote textbooks as well as poetry. When I think of North Carolinians, I love to think that the best known man in the world today is a North Carolinian. He preaches his heart out trying to get folks to accept Christ and to love the Lord, but instead of loving the Lord, they all fall in love with Billy Graham. Maybe not all, but many who brag about Billy Graham will not open their lips to say one word about Jesus.

Sir Walter loved his country and would, on many occasions, recount to me the many noble deeds of the founding fathers. Sir Walter was a patriot and was well-grounded in the basic principles of our liberty and freedom under the Constitution, but he also knew that the strength of this nation as a free people was based on what we place on our money as a motto, and not the money itself.

The strength of this nation is not in a great army, a great navy, a great air force, the atomic bomb, the H-bomb, a great missles force, or any other material thing; but the strength of this nation is our faith in God. And when I say faith in God I don't mean an abstract superficial sort of faith. I mean old-fashioned saving faith in the Lord Jesus Christ, who is God. I don't know of a single blood-bought, born-again Christian man in this country who is afraid of anything. He does not know what is ahead, but he knows *Who* is ahead. He does not know what the future holds, but he knows *Who* holds the future. The fear in the hearts of many Americans is a lack of old-fashioned faith. If the people of this nation would sincerely turn to God in faith, I believe that God himself would put a ring in the nose of Communism. Surely, it would take fear out of our hearts, and in simple childlike faith, we could look away to the blue and say in our hearts, "Let come what may, the Eternal God is our refuge and underneath are His everlasting arms."

Christianity is *not* a religion. It is a supernatural revelation from God. You cannot kill a Christian. Suppose you drop the atomic bomb on him, he is only then absent from the body and present with the Lord.

This old world has lost its way, but the Christian goes right on;
The world is lost in sin's dismay, but the Christian goes right on;
Temptations and trials and testings too, will prove what Christ can do for you;
Keep looking up, and smiling through, for the Christian goes right on, and on.
The Christian goes right on!

CALL YOUR NEXT CASE.